African Names

African Names

Names From the
African Continent
for Children
and Adults

by Julia Stewart

A Citadel Press Book
Published by Carol Publishing Group

In Memory of
ESTHER A. CURFMAN

Carol Publishing Group Edition, 1996

A Citadel Press Book
Published by Carol Publishing Group
Citadel Press is a registered trademark of Carol Communications, Inc.

For editorial, sales and distribution, and queries regarding rights and permissions, write to Carol Publishing Group, 120 Enterprise Avenue, Secaucus, N.J. 07094

In Canada: Canadian Manda Group, One Atlantic Avenue, Suite 105, Toronto, Ontario M6K 3E7

Carol Publishing Group books are available at special discounts for bulk purchases, sales promotions, fund-raising, or educational purposes. Special editions can also be created to specifications.

Interior illustrations by Todd H. Schaffer.

Manufactured in the United States of America
10 9 8 7 6 5 4

Library of Congress Cataloging-in-Publication Data

Stewart, Julia
    African names: names from the African continent for children and adults / by Julia Stewart.
        p. cm.
    "A Citadel Press book."
    ISBN 0-8065-1386-1
    1. Names, Personal —African—Dictionaries—English. 2. Names, Personal—Africa—Dictionaries—English. I. Title.
CS2375.A33S74   1993
929.4'096—dc20   93-9441
                                                      CIP

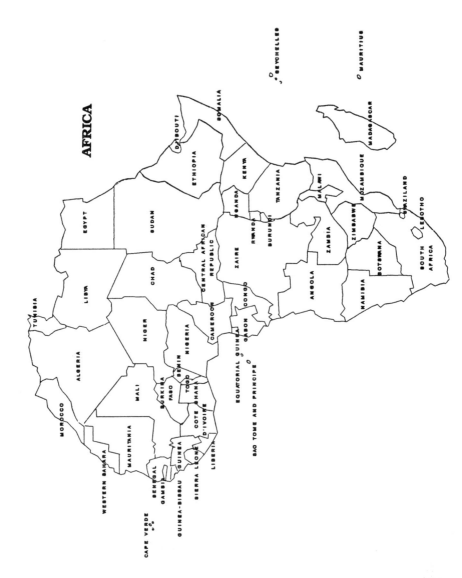

AFRICA

Introduction

These days African Americans are turning up the volume on who they are and where they came from. African names are a useful tool for this process. In spirit at least, the names that were stripped from African slaves to weaken their psyche are now being restored. Giving a child or yourself an ethnic name can be an important step in reaffirming cultural pride. Names are not just words, they are a link to all the ancestors who came before you and all the progeny who will follow. With the mere mention of an African name, one can conjure up images of vast savannas and endless deserts, dense forests and palm-fringed beaches, of golden ancient kingdoms and proud warriors, of spirited music and dance, of urban hustle-bustle, and rural tranquility. Most of all, one can imagine the smiling faces of children who will carry their revived ethnic traditions to the next generation.

Traditional African names have wonderful meanings and unique histories. One family from the eastern region of Ghana carries the surname Akrobettoe. The origin of the name traces back four or more generations to a great-great grandfather who lived among the Yilo-Krobo people. When another tribe threatened to wage war with the Krobos, most of the people fled. The grandfather declared he would stay to protect the chiefdom and that when the others returned they would find him alive. After the battle ended and the deserters returned, they found the man alive and made him Paramount Chief for showing such great courage. The new Paramount chief of the Yilo-Krobo people became known as Akrobettoe—"akro" literally meaning "one is leaving," and "bettoe" meaning "you will come back and meet me." Today the name signifies "formidable, strong."

People of African descent in the Americas have long been separated from the naming traditions of their motherland. Due to the severing of ancestral links during the days of slavery and the forced acceptance of names from the dominant culture, most African Americans carry names of European origin. Very few African Americans can trace their parentage back to Africa to recover old family names. Alex Haley, the author of *Roots*, succeeded in this, but certainly it involved considerable time and expense. Spending copious amounts of time and money to pinpoint one's roots is not a luxury available to most people.

The inability to establish the exact location in Africa from whence one's family originated is a two-sided coin. On the negative side, it is a constant reminder of the gross inhumanity of the slave trade which stripped people of all they possessed, even the ability to pass their ancestral names to their children. On the positive side, it unfolds the entire continent of Africa as a source of inspiration and a symbol of one's heritage, as opposed to one small corner of this immense and diverse land. Africans themselves rarely have the luxury of such a consolidated and romantic view of their continent.

In this respect, African Americans have the opportunity to be not only on the cutting edge of cultural revivalism in America, but throughout the African diaspora. Ali A. Mazrui writes in his book *The Africans: A Triple Heritage*:

... the Diaspora had been dis-Africanised by the West, and yet at the same time racialised in identity. 'Forget you are African, remember you are Black!' The African geographical and culture ancestry was originally suppressed among African sons and daughters of the Diaspora; while the focus of identity turned more firmly to the physical characteristic of being Black. But there are indications of a partial re-Africanisation in the Diaspora, of a search to re-create the myth of ancestry. With such a re-creation Africa could at last rediscover its bonds with those who were forcibly exported centuries ago.

It is unfortunate that many English language speakers believe it is too awkward to pronounce African names. True enough African names can be made up of multiple consonants, as in Nganga, Mwazwenyi, Msrah, and Tshekedi. Or they twist tongues with their length; try saying Keanyandaarwa and Mawulawde. Also true is the fact that bearers of complicated or unusual names can become exasperated by spending a lifetime repeating their own names five or six times at every introduction and spelling it over and over again for those who just can't get them right. But for every Keanyandaarwa and Mawulawde there is a Chanya and Juba—simple names to say and spell. With this book an attempt has been made to sort the simple and beautiful names from the longer ones. Although a few long and twisty names have been included for adventurous readers, possible nicknames are suggested.

The perceived pronunciation barrier may be one factor inhibiting people of African heritage who live in English-speaking countries from adopting, on a wide scale, names reflecting their African ancestry for themselves and their children. Other prohibitive factors could be the lack of comprehensive sources of African names and a shortage of popular information about the continent.

What a shame! Because the continent of Africa is overflowing with gorgeous names, charming and melodic names, even to the English-speaking ear. There are hundreds, even thousands, of towns and cities, rivers and lakes, ethnic peoples, ancient royalty and modern dignitaries of Africa with names that are hauntingly unforgettable; not to mention the countless, wonderful, traditional ethnic names.

If you balk at the idea of naming your little ones after a river or a town or an ethnic group, consider that many cultures, including those of Europe, have customarily derived personal names from place names, objects, and groups of people. For example, in Ghana the male name Offin comes from the name of the Offin River, while the English male name Wylie is from the Wiley River. For the Greeks, Magda means "woman from the city of Magdala" and Cyprian means "native of Cyprus." Kanika is a Kenyan name derived from the Kiswahili word for "dark cloth" and Portia is a Spanish name derived from the Latin word for "a port."

So try this name on for size: Naivasha. Naivasha is a scenic lake lying on the floor of the Great Rift Valley in Kenya. The lake's tranquility is overwhelming. It is a place where you can read, walk and think for days, leaving behind the tumultuous outside world. Birdlife at the lake has been known to make ornithologists swoon. From the lake's shore you can gaze at the monstrous hippo nostrils peeking out of the water and local fishermen on the dock catching spiny crayfish. At night you may hear the honking, grunting noises of hungry hippos who have come ashore to graze. The name Naivasha, as with the beauty and tranquility of the lake, has stuck indelibly in my mind since the first time I heard it. Naivasha—what a wonderful name for a baby girl, I thought. And really that is where this book began.

Whether you are of African ancestry, a student of Africa and its peoples, or you are merely looking for an unusual, enchanting, lyrical name, this book is for you.

Trends in Selecting Names

In traditional African cultures parents bestowed names upon newborn children that paid homage to the ancestors, appealed to the deities and spirits, evoked the status of the family, or bespoke the plight of the world around them.* Names also reflected the time when a child was born— whether in daylight or at nighttime, on market day or during a holy month, on Monday or on Wednesday. For example, a Dinka boy born in time of drought may have been called

---

* In regions of Africa where the Islamic religion predominates Muslim names tend to supersede traditional ethnic names, as they have for centuries.

Monyyak, literally "Man of the Drought." Swahili children born on Friday have been named Juma, derived from the Kiswahili word for that day, Ijumaa. The Ibibio and Efik peoples of Nigeria often named boys born on market day Edet, the word used for that day. Ezeji is a Nigerian male name, literally meaning "the King of Yams," which expresses that the family is well-off at the time because of their large supply of yams.

With the rapid changes of the twentieth century, name giving in many African societies has detoured from traditional patterns. Due to the strong influence of Christianity on the continent, it has become common for Africans to adopt Christian forenames—meaning western names—be they French, Portuguese, Spanish, Italian, or English. In Nairobi, the capital of Kenya, men called Francis and Simon and women who answer to the names of Joyce and Mary are a dime a dozen. The Francophone names Michel, Sandrine, Justine, and Pascal can be heard on the streets of Zaire. Then there is the case of the little girl in a remote village in Zaire whose parents named her Pencil. In her corner of the world the object after which she's named is something modern and valuable. And the name, pronounced with a French accent, does have a nice ring to it.

Having said this, it is notable that many African ethnic groups retain traditional name-giving patterns. For example, it is still common in Ghana to name children according to the day of the week on which they were born or by the order of their birth, as in Manu meaning "second born." Meanwhile, some urban, educated African parents with Christian names are rediscovering the beauty and significance of ancestral names and those of other African ethnic groups. In many instances they are choosing these names over Western ones for their children. Like everyone else throughout the world, Africans must balance their traditional customs and the desire for cultural preservation with modern pressures and realities.

In the cultural hodgepodge that is North America, we depend primarily on last names to indicate a person's ethnic or geographic origin. The McKirgan family we know has Irish ancestors; the Chen's are from China; the Hernandez family is Latin American. In contrast, first names are not usually dictated by lineage, but instead are influenced by the predominant culture. It could be Suzie Chen, Suzie McKirgan, or Suzie Hernandez. Adopting mainstream first names or simplifying ethnic names is common practice in multi-ethnic communities; it helps to assimilate peoples into society.

African Americans are the exception to this rule. People of African origin constitute about 13 percent of the population of the United States, but can you think of one African surname? Unlike virtually all other ethnic groups, African Americans hold both first and last names representative of the predominant culture. Technically then, African Americans should consider changing their family names and continue to use first names common to our part of the world, in the same vein as Suzie Chen. However, being in a unique situation demands a unique response.

For African Americans the split from ancestral roots was so drastic and occurred so long ago that concessions can be made to current realities. Changing the surname of an entire family may present complications. It would mean foregoing the names borne by ancestors over the past few generations; it could cause complications with regard to current family ties; and legally it would be more difficult than simply adopting new first names.

Bestowing ethnic first and middle names on your children or yourself may be easier and can serve the same purpose of cultural affirmation. Take the example of African-American storyteller Phillip Sekou Glass. He is able to retain his family name, use a mainstream first name, and still declare his ancestral heritage through that one name—Sekou. However, for those interested in tackling a family-name change, there is a list of African surnames in the Appendixes. Keep in mind this list is only a drop in the ocean in comparison to the thousands of surnames used on the African continent. You may be able to get further lists from the embassies of specific

African countries. Also, note that many African cultures do not have the same concept of forenames and surnames that we have. Second names are not always family names but may be a father's given name, as for example is customary in Ethiopia, and therefore would be used only one generation.

No matter which name you choose, Leonard R. N. Ashley, author of *What's In A Name?*, advises to keep it short and avoid names that are difficult to spell. He also suggests that you should imagine the name being used in different circumstances. For example, envision an elementary school teacher calling on your child to answer a question. How does "Dessie, tell us who was the first president of Kenya" sound? Or, "Danso, what is ten times twelve?"

The Legalities of Changing Your Name

You can change your name from Tom Brown to Manas Koroli or Diane Jones to Jina Mandela in the blink of an eye. For adults to change their names in most states the legal requirement is simply consistent use of the new name, of course without fraudulent intent. However, if you feel confident that your new name is going to be with you for the foreseeable future, consider obtaining a court order to avoid complications.

You must obtain a court order to change children's names and in some states both parents must agree on this change.

To obtain a court order contact your County Probate Court. The process should not be difficult to complete although it may take some time. In Ohio, for example, you must go to the probate court with identification, fill out paperwork, and pay a fee of approximately eighty dollars. A court hearing date will be set for four to six weeks later. After the hearing your name change is recorded in court records and notice of the change is attached to your birth certificate. Then you are responsible for notifying agencies that have issued your official documents, such as driver's license, auto title, social security card, credit cards, IRS, bank accounts, passport, etc.

Understanding the Book

The continent of Africa is now made up of fifty-two countries. Its land area is three times the size of the United States. African history reaches back to the very first days of humankind and includes some of the planet's most impressive kingdoms.

Africa's people are a diverse group. The continent is home to more than one thousand ethnic groups speaking hundreds of languages consisting of thousands of dialects. Outside of, and even within Africa itself, many of the names of these peoples, their languages, and their countries, are unknown. Many of Africa's magnificent natural wonders also remain in obscurity to much of the world. This book attempts to bring some of those people, places and aspects of Africa out of the shadows.

African Languages

Hundreds of different languages, and thousands of dialects of those languages, are spoken on the African continent. These languages can be broken down into six major language families: Bantu, with 182 different languages; Semitic, with ten languages; Hamitic, with some 47 languages; Hottentot; Sudanic, with 264 different languages; and Bushman, having 11 languages. In addition, French, English, Spanish, Portuguese, Afrikaans, and Arabic are spoken. All of these languages have had an effect on place names and personal names used in Africa.

Below is a list of the major indigenous languages spoken in Africa. Included, where known, are estimates of the number of speakers and areas where the languages are primarily spoken. Estimates of the numbers of speakers vary greatly from source to source, so this is by no means a definitive list.

West African Languages:

AHANTA	Ghana, Cote D'Ivoire
BAMBARA	Francophone West Africa
BASSA	Liberia, Cameroon
DIOULA	Burkina Faso, Cote D'Ivoire
EFIK	Nigeria (est. 1 million speakers)
EWE (POPO)	Ghana, Togo, Benin (est. 3 million speakers)
FANG	Equatorial Guinea (est. 2 million speakers)
FON	Benin, Togo (est. 1 million speakers)
FULANI (FULFULDE)	Nigeria, Niger (est. 10 million speakers)
HAUSA	Nigeria, Niger, Ghana (est. 30 million speakers)
IBO (IGBO)	Nigeria (est. 10 million speakers)
KPELLE	Liberia (est. .5 million speakers)
KRU	Liberia, Cote D'Ivoire
MALINKE (MANDINKA)	Francophone West Africa (est. 10 million speakers)
MENDE	Sierra Leone (est. 1 million speakers)
MOSSI (MORE)	Francophone West Africa (est. 3 million speakers)
SARAKOLLE (SONINKE)	Mali, Burkina Faso, Mauritania
SONGHAI	Nigeria (est. 1 million speakers)

TWI (AKAN)	Ghana, Cote D'Ivoire (est. 4 million speakers)
WOLOF	Senegal, Gambia, Mauritania, Equatorial Guinea (est. 2 million speakers)
YORUBA	Benin, Togo, Nigeria (est. 17 million speakers)

North African Languages:

BARI	Sudan
BERBER	North Africa (est. 10 million speakers)
DINKA	Sudan
NUBA	Nile region below Aswan

East and Central African Languages:

AFAR	Ethiopia, Djibouti, Somalia (est. .5 million speakers)
AMHARIC (AMARINYA)	Ethiopia (est. 12 million speakers)
KAMBA	Kenya (est. 1 million speakers)
KIBUNDU	Angola (est. 2 million speakers)
KIKUYU	Kenya (est. 2.5 million speakers)
KILUBA	Zaire (est. 3 million speakers)
KIKONGO	Zaire (est. 3 million speakers)
KINYARWANDA	Rwanda (est. 5 million speakers)
KIRUNDI	Burundi (est. 4 million speakers)
KISWAHILI	East Africa (est. 20-60 million speakers)
LINGALA	Zaire (est. 10 million speakers)
LUGANDA	Uganda (est. 2 million speakers)
OROMO	Ethiopia (est. 10 million speakers)
SANGO	Central African Republic (est. 2 million speakers)
SOMALI	Somalia, Kenya (est. 6 million speakers)
UMBUNDU	Angola (est. 2 million speakers)

Southern African Languages

BEMBA	Zambia (est. 1.5 million speakers)
HERERO	Namibia
HOTTENTOT	Namibia, South Africa
MALAGASY	Madagascar (est. 8 million speakers)
NYANJA-CHICHEWA	Zambia, Malawi (est. 4 million speakers)
SESOTHO	Lesotho, South Africa, Swaziland
SHONA	Zimbabwe (est. 4 million speakers)
SISWATI	Swaziland (est. 1 million speakers)
SETSWANA	Botswana (est. 2.5 million speakers)
XHOSA	South Africa (est. 4 million speakers)
ZULU	South Africa (est. 4 million speakers)

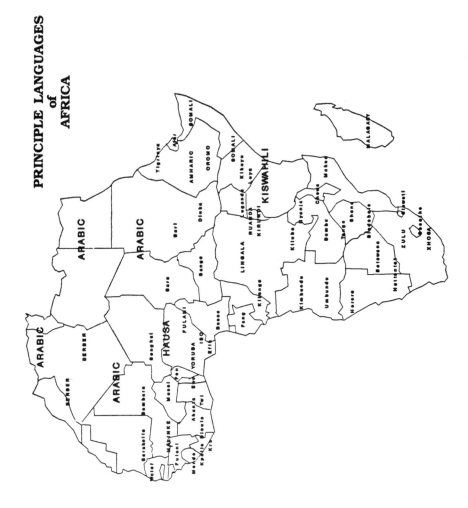

PRINCIPLE LANGUAGES
of
AFRICA

The language group most likely to spark reader recognition is the Bantu language family. This group includes Kiswahili, one of the most internationally recognizable African languages. Bantu languages are spoken throughout central, eastern, and southern Africa. They originated in central Africa, possibly in Cameroon, nearly five thousand years ago, and over the millenniums Bantu-speaking peoples migrated to the east and south of the continent. Bantu languages spoken today include Bemba, Chokwe, Fang, Herero, Kamba, Kikongo, Kikuyu, Kiswahili, Luganda, Mbuti, Ndebele, Rwanda, Rundi, Sesotho, Setswana, Siswazi, Venda, Xhosa, and Zulu.

Swahili Culture and Kiswahili Language

Let me first acknowledge that there is indeed a heavy concentration of Swahili and East African names in the book due to the author's own experience and resources of that region of the continent. Don't forget that Africa is three times the size of the United States, so becoming knowledgeable about every region of this vast land requires a lifetime of study.

The word Kiswahili refers to a language. This should be distinguished from the word Swahili which refers to a culture and its people. The Swahili people live mainly along the East African coast. They are a mix of indigenous African and Arab races who look more African than Arabic, though most follow the Islamic religion and lead a Muslim lifestyle. It was through the Swahili that the Kiswahili language developed and spread throughout eastern Africa over many centuries.

Kiswahili is one of Africa's best known and most widely spoken languages. Estimates of the total number of Kiswahili speakers range from twenty–sixty million people. Most Kiswahili speakers are found in Kenya, Tanzania and Uganda, although Kiswahili is spoken as far south as South African port cities and as far north as the Arabic country of Oman.

Kiswahili is based on Bantu, an indigenous African language family, and is heavily influenced by Arabic and English, as well as some Portuguese and German (albeit in eastern Zaire it is heavily influenced by French). Modern notions and technical words are easily "Kiswahilized," as with the words helikopta for helicopter, koti for coat, and gari for car, which allows Kiswahili to grow with the times. In part, because of this ability to adopt easily to a rapidly modernizing world, Kiswahili has spread throughout East Africa as a trade language used by a wide variety of ethnic groups as a means of communication across cultures.

Muslim Names

Quite a few Muslim names appear in this book. Africa, from the Sahara Desert northwards, is almost entirely Islamic and is generally considered more a part of the Arab world than Africa. A heavy Muslim influence exists in sub-Sahara Africa as well, where at least fifteen countries have a Muslim majority. Approximately one-fourth of the pilgrims making the hajj to Mecca each year come from the African continent.

It is not uncommon for African Americans to adopt Muslim names, as did sports stars Muhammad Ali and Kareem Abdul-Jabbar. At times, however, this can be confusing. If you read the name Khalid Muhammed in the newspaper, what would you assume? First, you might guess that the subject is Muslim. Secondly, he may be of Arab descent, perhaps from Saudi Arabia or Lebanon. It is only when you find out that he lives in a predominantly black neighborhood that you realize he is an African American. But if you read the names John Luthuli, or Mogo Luthuli, or Luthuli Johnson, you immediately visualize a man from Africa, either an African or an African American.

In this book an attempt was made to limit Muslim names to those which relate to prominent African figures or those which are notably popular in an African country. For example, you will find the names Ismail, an eighteenth-century king of Abyssinia (modern-day Ethiopia), Sulaiman, and Halima, popular Muslim names in North Africa.

Selection of Names for This Book

Names were chosen for this book based primarily on the aesthetics of sound. They had to be relatively easy to pronounce for English speakers and at the same time be memorable and meaningful. Some, although a bit uncomfortable to the English speaker's ear, were added because of their historical or cultural significance.

Some names, like Betsimisaraka, seem to violate the advice given earlier that names should be kept short. In these cases short forms of the names are suggested at the end of the definition. Thus, Betsimisaraka can be shortened to Betsi or Misaraka. Or the child's first name could be Betsi and the middle name might be Misaraka.

Gender of Names

The names are categorized by gender. However, again the deciding factor was sound. Names like Naivasha and Najaca, the former the name of a lake and the latter the name of a village, sound feminine and thus are listed under female. In fact, most of the names ending in "a" are listed as female. Although many African male names end in "a," in English-speaking countries, male names rarely do. The goal of this book is to make these names work in our English-language environment.

However, names need not be limited to the gender under which they are listed. It is up to the reader to decide. The only names that might best remain gender specific are those whose definition explicitly refers to a gender according to a particular culture.

Explore a New Meaning for Your Present Name

I already have a name, you might say. And frankly, you might add, I like it! You could be surprised to discover that some contemporary western names have meaning in Africa. Review the following list of names that appear in this book. One of them may be yours. Look it up; your name may have a significance you never imagined.

ADA, ADRIAN, ALEXANDRIA, ANNA, ANTHONY, AUGUSTINE, BARRY, BO, BONNY, CANDACE, CHAD, CONSTANTINE, DAN, DON, EVA, HOGAN, JULIUS, KIM, LEA, LINDA, LISA, LOLA, LULU, MIMI, MONA, MONICA, MOSES, PETE, PIA, RHODA, RON, SARA, TERA, TERENCE, THEODORE (look under Tewodros), VICTORIA, WANDA.

Convert Your Present Name to an African Variation

Some contemporary English names can easily be converted simply by changing a letter here or there. This allows you to retain the basis of the name bestowed upon you by your parents (which they may have agonized long and hard to select), and still reflect your cultural heritage. English names that could be transformed to African names found in this book are listed below.

Abe to ABERASHID, ABEBE
Adam to ADOM
Al to ALADIAN
Amanda to MANDA, MANDARA
Ann, Anne to ANNABA
Ashley to ASHIA, AISHA
Barbara to BARA, BARAKA
Ben to BENI, BENGHAZI, BENDEL
Bernard to BERHANU
Bertha to BERTA

Betty, Betsy to BETI, BETSIMISARAKA, BETSIBOKA
Cal, Calvin to KALENJIN
Cora to KORA
Dan, Daniel to DANAKIL, DANSO
Darin, Darren, Daryl, Darrell to DAREN
David to DAUDI, DAWIT, DAVIE
Debbie to DEBBA, DEBRE BERHAN, DEBRE DAMO,
    DEBRE MARKOS
Della to DELA O KANDE
Di, Didi to DIDYME, DIDESSA
Dionne, Diane, Diana to DYAN, DIANI
Don. Dom to DOMEVLO
Effy to EFE, EFFIWAT, EFIA
Gabby, Gabriella to GABRI, GABBRA
Gary to GARIAN
Ginger to JINJA
Harry, Harrison to HERI
Janet to DJANET, JANA
Jeane to JINA, JINI
Jim to JIMBO
Jo, Joseph to JOJO, JOMO, JOS, JOZI
John, Jonathan to YOHANNES, YOHANCE
Julie, Julia to TULI, TULIA, JOLIBA
Kay to KAYLA
Karen, Carrie, Caroline to KARI, KARIN, KARA, KERA,
    KEREN, KERAN
Katherine to KASSERINE
Kim to KIMBAVETA
Kurt, Curtis to KURTEY
Larry, Lawrence to LARI, LERIBE
Laura to LAWRA
Lindy, Lindie to MALINDI, LINDIWE, LINDI
Lisa to LISALA, LISSAWAN
Lori to LORIAN
Margy, Margaret, Marge, Majorie to MARGI, MARGAI
Maria to MARI

Mariam to MARIAMA
Marty to MARTI
Mary Jane to MARJANI
Merrill to MERILLE
Mike, Michael to MIKEA
Monroe to MONROVIA
Ray to REY MALABO, RESHE
Rueben to RUBANI
Rudy, Rudolph to RUDI, RUDO
Sam to SAMBURU, SAMORI
Sandy, Sandra to SASSANDRA, SANDI
Sara, Sarah to SARAKOLE, SAHARA, SARAKAWA
Sheila to SHILA, SHELLA
Sherman to SHERBRO, SHERMARKE
Sherry to SHARI
Sissy to SISAY, SISI
Sonny to SONNI ALI
Sue, Susan, Suzanne to SU, SUDIE, SUSA
Tobias, Toby to TOBECHUKWU
Tonya to FANYA, TANA
Tim to TEM
Tina to TINI, TIMA
Tommy, Tom to TOMI
Vince to VINZA
Wally, Walter to WALI
Wanda to RWANDA

Those Fun, Goofy, Nicknames for Your Child, a Friend, a Pet

Some of the names found within these pages have a bouncy, informal feel, making them especially suitable to use as nicknames—those sweet names we bestow upon loved ones whether they are a toddler, friend, athlete, or pet. Here are some potential nicknames.

BABA	JIMBO	PUPA
BIBI	KOKO	SHUBI
BOBO	KRESH	SISI
BUPE	KUKU	TAFI
COCO	KWEKWE	TATA
DADA	MTOTO	TINI
FANG	PILIPILI	TUMTUM
GOGO	POPO	UCHI
		WANKIE

Pronunciation Guide for This Book

The majority of the names in this book are followed by a pronunciation enclosed in parentheses. The phonetics are intended to make pronunciation as easy as possible.

Some African languages have sounds unfamiliar to English speakers, like the click sounds in various southern African languages, or the throaty sounds of languages influenced by Arabic. Therefore, although attempts were made to be as accurate as possible, some names will be pronounced in a way that may not be an exact ethnic pronunciation, but rather one that English speakers can understand.

The following is a list of symbols used in this book followed by examples of the sounds used in English words. The stressed syllable in each word will be indicated by capital letters, such as MOH-goh.

Book Symbols	Example
ah	father
a	pat
ay	pay
uh	about, **gut**
air	**care, air**
eh	met
ee	bee
i	fit
igh	**high**
eer	**pier**
oh	toe
o	hot
oo	boot, **fruit**
aw	**paw, brawl**
oy	**toy, noise**
u	put
ur	batt**er**
s	yes
j	jelly
g	**go**
z	**zoo**
th	**thing**

Further Research

Some readers may be interested in doing additional research on names found in this book. Others might like to search for their own unique African name. For those so inclined, refer to the Appendixes in the back of the book. These lists may be a useful beginning for your research.

Acknowledgments

I would like to express gratitude to the following beings for making this book a possibility: John Tawia Akrobettoe and his network of African friends in Columbus, Ohio, for help with West African names; Jima A. Dula and his cohorts in Los Angeles for going beyond the call of friendship in helping with Ethiopian names; Marwan Shiblaq for help with Arabic pronunciations; Julie Wright for helping with southern African names; Sarah Johnston, Professor of Classics at Ohio State University; my friends and colleagues in Nairobi, Kenya—Hawa Matiku, Joyce Boshosho, Kalume, Japhed Mahagwa, and Peter Odero; Diane Nell and Ivor Melmor for assistance with Somali names; Susan Tsiangalara, Education Officer for the Embassy of Madagascar; Togo Mission to the United Nations; Embassy of the Sudan; Embassy of Mali; Embassy of Algeria; Todd Schaffer for inestimable amounts of support, both financial and emotional; Jaqueline Brown for being there at the inception of this project (although petering out on the follow through!); Bongo for being a good dog; and Allan J. Wilson, editor at Carol Publishing, for finding merit in this work.

Personal names are inseparable from the issue of identity in human affairs.
—ALI MAZRUI, *The Africans: A Triple Heritage*

Cross of Dese

Cross of Jima

Cross of Zinder

African Names

A

The world is a beehive; everyone enters through the same door.

—African Proverb

Female

ABA (AH-buh)   A city in southeastern Nigeria near Port Harcourt. Also, a town in northeastern Zaire near the border with Sudan.

ABBA (AHB-bah)   Ghanaian name for females born on Thursday.

ABEBA (ah-beh-BAH)   Ethiopian female name meaning "flower."

ABEBI (ah-BAY-bee)   Yoruba of Nigeria female name meaning "we asked and got her" or "we asked for her and she came to us."

ABENA (ah-BEE-nah)   Akan of Ghana name for females born on Tuesday.

ABRIHET (ahb-ruh-HUHT)   Tigrinya of Ethiopia female name meaning "she has made it light, she emanates light."

ACACIA (uh-KAY-shuh)   a) A tropical tree with branches spreading wide and flat. Also called a thorn tree, it is commonly seen on African savannas. The Acacia tree represents life after death and immortality. b) A Greek female name meaning "thorny."

ACHAN   Dinka of south Sudan name for a female child in the first pair of twins.

3

ADA a) (ah-DAH) Ibo of Nigeria name for firstborn females. b) (AH-dah) A Kiswahili word meaning "fee." c) (AY-da) A town in southeast Ghana at the mouth of the Volta River. d) (ah-DAH) A Hebrew female name meaning "beauty, pleasure"; there are two women named Ada found in the bible, the wife of Lamech and the wife of Esau. e) (AY-duh) Female name derived from either Teutonic meaning "happy," or Latin meaning "of noble birth."

ADAMA (ah-DAHM-ah) Ibo of Nigeria female name meaning "beautiful child" or "queenly."

ADANECH (ah-DAH-nehtch) Amharic and Tigrinya of Ethiopia female name meaning "she has rescued them."

ADANNA (ah-DAHN-ah) Ibo of Nigeria female name meaning "father's daughter."

ADEOLA (ah-day-OH-lah) Yoruba of Nigeria female name meaning "crown has honor."

ADINA a) (AH-duh-nah) Amharic of Ethiopia word, which is sometimes used as a female name, meaning "she has saved." b) (ah-DEE-nah) Tigrinya of Ethiopia word meaning "our country." c) (ah-dee-NAH) Hebrew female name meaning "voluptuous, adorned."

ADJOA (AH-joh-ah) Also spelled **ADWOA**, an Akan of Ghana name for females born on Monday.

AFAFA (ah-FAH-fah) Ewe of Ghana female name for the firstborn child of a second husband.

AFIA (eh-FEE-ah) Akan of Ghana name for females born on Friday.

AFIYA (ah-FEE-yah) Another spelling for the Swahili female name AFYA (see below).

AFRA (AHF-ruh) a) Name meaning "peaceful ruler" used by ancient Romans and Greeks for females of African origin. b) Muslim female name meaning "earth colored." c) Hebrew female name meaning "young deer."

AFRICA (AF-ree-kuh) Accounts vary on the origin of the name of the continent of Africa. Some believe it refers to the name of an ancient Berber peoples who inhabited North Africa; others believe Africa means "greyish" in reference

4

to the color of sand; yet another theory is that it is a Phoenician word meaning "colony," since North Africa was once a colony of the Roman Empire. Spelled **AFFRICA,** it is a female name used in Spanish-speaking countries, meaning "pleasant."

AFYA (AHF-yah)   Swahili female name and Kiswahili word meaning "health." Afya Bora (BOHR-ah) means "good health."

AGBENYAGA (ahg-BAY-nyah-gah)   Ewe of Ghana name meaning "life is precious." (Could be shortened to **NYAGA.**)

AGNI (AHG-nee)   a) A people and language of Cote D'Ivoire, related to the Ashanti. The Agni are believed to have Egyptian origins. b) In India Agni is the mythological god of fire. His name comes from the Latin word "ignis," meaning fire.

AHANTA (ah-HAHN-tah)   A people and language of Ghana and Cote D'Ivoire. From the Kwa language family, Ahanta is a dialect of Anyi (Agni).

AINA (ah-ee-NAH)   Yoruba of Nigeria female name meaning "difficult birth."

AISHA (ah-EE-shah, AH-ee-shuh)   Also spelled **AYISHA** and **ASHA** (AH-shah), this Swahili and Arabic female name means "life, alive" and refers to the Muslim Prophet Muhammed's chief wife.

AKIM (ah-KEEM)   According to an Ibibio of Nigeria folktale, Akim was a gorgeous, fat, young woman made of oil who melted in the sun while doing farm labor. Also, Akim is the name of a town in Ghana and of a Twi-speaking people, known in full as Akim Abuakwa (ahb-WAH-kwa), or the Akims.

AKINA (ah-KEE-nah)   The Kiswahili word for "relations, connections." Akina Mama is translated as "women folk." The Akina Mama wa Africa (Solidarity of African Women) is a London-based African women's group. Also, Akina is a Japanese female name meaning "bright flower."

AKOSUA (ah-koh-SOO-ah)   Akan of Ghana name for females born on Sunday.

AKPENAMAWU (ahk-PAY-nah-MAH-woo)   Ewe of Ghana name meaning "thanks to God." The Ghanaian short form of this name is **AKPENA** (ahk-PAY-nah).

AKUA (eh-KWEE-ah)   Akan of Ghana name for females born on Wednes.

ALEXANDRIA (AL-ig-ZAN-dree-uh)   Also called **ALEX-ANDRA**. a) The chief port city of Egypt, where the Nile River finds outlet into the Mediterranean Sea. Alexandria was founded in 332 B.C. by Alexander the Great and was Egypt's capital for over one thousand years. It was the world's center of culture and learning during the Ptolemaic dynasty (323–30 B.C.). Scholars the world over travelled to this city to study in Greek and Coptic languages at the Library of Alexandria. b) Alexandra is the female version of the Greek name Alexander, meaning "helper of mankind." (May be shortened to **ALEX, ALEXIS, ALI** or **ANDRIA**.)

ALITASH (AH-luh-tash)   Amharic of Ethiopia female name meaning "may I not lose you, may I find you always my precious." (May be shortened to **TASH**.)

ALOME (ah-loh-MAY)   Alome is the original name of the city of Lome, capital of Togo. The city, founded over two hundred years ago by a man named Djitri, earned the name Alome because of the presence of aloe twigs, which were and still are used as natural toothbrushes.

AMA (AH-mah)   a) Also spelled **AMMA**. Akan people of Ghana name for females born on Saturday. b) West African name meaning "happy." c) An Efik word meaning "beloved." d) The Kiswahili word for "either, or." e) Ama A. Aidoo is a Ghanaian short-story writer and dramatist whose works include *Our Sister Killjoy* and *Sunset in Biafra.*

AMANISHAKHETE (ah-MAHN-ee-shahk-HAY-tay)   The name of one of the Candaces, or Queen Mothers, of the Nubian kingdom of Kush (now northern Sudan). (This name could be shortened to **AMANI** (ah-MAHN-ee), itself a Kiswahili word meaning "peace.")

AMARA (ahm-AHR-ah)   In the legends of Abyssinia (now Ethiopia) Amara is the name for paradise. Also, "amara" is a Kiswahili word meaning "urgent business."

AMARINYA (ah-mahr-IN-yah)   Amarinya is the locally used name for the language spoken in Shoa Province, Ethiopia. More widely known as Amharic, it is the official language of Ethiopia, spoken by some twenty-five million people as a first or second language.

AMBER (AM-bur)   Muslim female name meaning "amber, brownish-yellow," or "jewel." Amber is a semi-precious fossil resin that is believed to have the power to heal. Amber is widely used in making African jewelry and is coveted by Somali women.

AMHARA (ahm-HAHR-ah)   The Amhara people inhabit the north-central highlands of Ethiopia and number about twelve million. They speak a Semitic language called Amharic, which is Ethiopia's official language. (See AMARINYA.)

AMINA (ah-MEE-nah)   a) Somali and Muslim female name meaning "trustful, honest" and referring to Muhammed's mother. This name is popular with the Hausa of West Africa. b) A Mende word meaning "amen."

AMINATA (ah-mee-NAH-tah)   A popular female name among the Wolof of Senegal. In 1976, Aminata Sow-Fall became the first woman in Francophone sub-Sahara Africa to publish a novel, called *Le Revenant.*

AMINIA (ah-meen-EE-ah)   A Kiswahili word meaning "to believe in."

ANDROMEDA (an-DROM-uh-duh)   "Ruler of men." According to Greek mythology, Andromeda married Perseus, who had saved her from Medusa, a monster of the sea. Andromeda was said to be an Aethiopian (meaning African) princess. Ancient Aethiopians considered Perseus and Andromeda the progenitors of the black race.

ANNA (AH-nah)   The name Anna is applied to those Hausa people of Nigeria who have maintained traditional societal practices and religious beliefs. They are generally thought of as poor, country folk of pagan (meaning non-Muslim) beliefs. Also, a popular female name of Hebrew origin meaning "gracious."

ANNABA (uh-NAHB-uh, an-NAHB-uh)   A large coastal city in northeastern Algeria with a busy natural harbor.

ANNAKIYA (AH-nah-KEE-yah)   This means "sweet face" in Hausa language.

ANTANANARIVO (AN-tuh-NAN-uh-REE-voh)   A Malagasy word meaning "at the place of a thousand warriors." Also called **TANANARIVE** (tuh-NAN-uh-REEV), this is the capital city of Madagascar. It is found in the island country's interior and is built on seven hills. The city is often referred to in short as **TANA** (TA-nuh), which means "place" or "town."

APHRODITE (AF-ruh-DIGH-tee)   The mythological Greek goddess of love and beauty who is sometimes depicted as being of black African origin. Venus is her equivalent in Roman literature. Aphrodite means "born of the foam of the sea."

APOLLONIA (AP-uh-LOH-nee-uh)   "Of Apollo." An ancient town in northern Libya on the Mediterranean Sea near the modern city of Marsa Susa. Older than 600 B.C., Apollonia was an important city of the Roman Empire. It was called **SOZUSA** during the Byzantine period.

ARET (ahr-EHT)   Ibibio of Nigeria name for female children born on market day, called Edet.

ARLIT (ahr-LEET)   Arlit is a town in the Sahara Desert in northern Niger. It is an important uranium mining town located in the Air (pronounced eye-ear) Mountains, which are about 6,600 feet (2,000 meters) high.

ARTEMIS (AHR-tuh-mis)   In Greek mythology, Artemis is goddess of the moon and the hunt. She is known as "the lady of wild things." This virgin goddess, who is sometimes depicted as being black African, is Apollo's twin sister. Artemis means "source of water."

ARUSHA (uh-ROO-shuh)   A city in northern Tanzania at the foot of Mount Meru and not far from Mount Kilimanjaro. This is a popular staging point for tourists on safaris in Tanzania. It also happens to be the half-way point on the road from Cape Town—the southernmost large city of Africa—to Cairo, Egypt in the north.

ARUSI a) (ah-ROO-see) Swahili name for girls born at the time of a wedding. "Arusi" is the Kiswahili word for wedding. b) (uh-ROO-see) A mountainous province of central Ethiopia with Asela as its capital.

ASHAKI (ah-SHAH-kee) West African female name meaning "beautiful."

ASHANTI (uh-SHAHN-tee) a) Also called the **ASANTE**, these Akan people live in south-central Ghana and Cote D'Ivoire. They are agriculturalists and speak the Twi language. b) The historic Ashanti kingdom (seventeenth to nineteenth centuries) covered all of present-day Ghana plus portions of Togo and Cote D'Ivoire. The kingdom drew its wealth from controlling trade in the area, particularly the gold trade. Kumasi, the kingdom's capital, paralleled European cities of the same time in its level of development. c) A region of central Ghana. This hilly area is traversed by the Afram, Oda and Offin rivers.

ASHIA (ASH-ee-uh) Somali female name referring to the prophet Muhammed's favorite wife.

ASKIYA (ahs-KEE-yah) Also spelled **ASKIA**, the name given to emperors of the Songhai Empire during the Askia Dynasty (A.D. 1493–1591). The Songhai Empire (A.D. 1350–1600) eclipsed the earlier Mali Empire and reached from the Atlantic Ocean in the west into present-day Nigeria in the east.

ASMARA (ahs-MAHR-ah) Capital city and commercial center of Eritrea (a contested region of northern Ethiopia). The city, sometimes spelled **ASMERA**, sits at an elevation of 7,500 feet (2,286 meters).

ASMINA (ahs-MEEN-ah) Female name of the Nubian peoples of southern Sudan.

ASURA (ah-SHOOR-ah) Swahili and Hausa name for female children born during the Muslim month of Ashur.

ATHI (A-thee) Athi River is the name of both a river and a town south of Nairobi, Kenya's capital. It is an important crossroads town and producer of cement.

ATSUKPI (ah-CHOO-pee) Ewe of Ghana name for a female twin.

9

AURORA (aw-RAWR-uh, uh-RAWR-uh) "Dawn." According to ancient Greek mythology, Aurora is the goddess of the dawn. Aurora was mother of Memnon, King of Aethiopia, whose African troops came to the aid of the Trojans at Troy. She is also known as **EOS** (EE-os).

AYAN (ah-YAHN) Somali female name meaning "bright."

AYANA (ah-YAHN-ah) Ethiopian female name meaning "beautiful flower."

AZANIA (uh-ZAYN-ee-uh) The east coast of East Africa was known by this name beginning in the first century A.D. Azania is the African name for the country of South Africa.

AZINZA (ah-ZEEN-zah) The word for "mermaid" in the Mina language of Togo.

AZIZA (ah-ZEE-zah, a-ZEE-zuh) Female name used in four languages: in Arabic and Kiswahili it means "precious;" in Somali it means "gorgeous;" in Hebrew it means "strong." Aziza is a popular name in Egypt.

AZMERA (ahz-MAIR-ah) Male and female name in both Amharic and Tigrinya languages of Ethiopia. It means "harvest."

Male

ABAI (AH-bigh) The name for the Nile River in the Amharic language of Ethiopia.

ABASI (ah-BAH-see) Swahili male name meaning "stern."

ABDALLA (ahb-DAHL-lah) A Swahili male name. It is a variant of the Arabic name **ABDULLAH**, which means "servant of God" and is popular in Egypt.

ABDELAHI (ahb-deh-LAH-hee) Muslim male name that is popular in Somalia.

ABDI (AB-dee) Muslim male name that is very popular in Somalia. It means "my servant."

ABDIKARIM (ahb-dee-kah-REEM) Muslim male name popular in Somalia that means "slave of God."

ABDIMELECH (AHB-dee-MEHL-ehk) An Aethiopian (meaning black African) eunuch who lived in ancient Rome.

The name means "servant to kings." (Could be shortened to **ABDI** or **MELECH**.)

ABDIRAXMAN (ahb-dee-RAH-mahn)   Somali version of the Muslim male name **ABD AL RAHMAN**, which means "servant of the Mercifully Gracious." This is a popular name in Somalia.

ABEBE (ah-BUH-buh)   Amharic of Ethiopia male name meaning "he has flowered/flourished/grown." Abebe Bikila (1932–1973) was born in Mout Province, Ethiopia. The eyes of the world fell on Abebe during the 1960 Olympics in Rome, where he won a gold medal for the marathon with a record-breaking time 2:15:16.2—which Abebe ran in bare feet. He again captured a gold medal in the marathon in the 1964 Olympics in Tokyo, beating his own record and making him the first man to win that title twice.

ABERASHID (ab-ur-ah-SHEED)   Aberashid Ali Shermarke became the first prime minister of Somalia in 1960. He became president of Somalia in 1967, but was assassinated soon thereafter. Aberashid held a Ph.D. in Political Science from Rome University.

ABRAFO (ah-BRAH-foh)   A Ghanaian male name meaning "warrior" or "executioner." It is not commonly given at birth; rather it is a nickname for someone who is hyper or a trouble-maker.

ADAN (ah-DAHN)   Yoruba of Nigeria male name meaning "a large bat." Also, a Spanish male name referring to the biblical Adam.

ADEN (AYD-n)   The Gulf of Aden is the western extension of the Arabian Sea and is geologically part of the Great Rift Valley. It is bordered by the African countries of Somalia and Djibouti, and by the Arabian Peninsula. The name is of Arabic origin and means "saddle."

ADLAN (ad-LAN)   Also **ADELAN**. In the eighteenth century, Sheikh Adlan was a vizier (important government official in Muslim societies) to King Ismail of the empire of Sennar. Sennar was located along the Blue Nile in Abyssinia (now Ethiopia).

ADOFO (ah-DOH-foh) Akan of Ghana male name meaning "one who loves."

ADOM (ah-DOHM) Akan of Ghana male name meaning "help from God" or "God's blessing."

ADRIAN (ah-dree-AHN, AY-dree-uhn) a) Name used for the nobility class of the Betsileo people of central Madagascar. b) Six Catholic popes have been named Adrian. c) A male name of Latin origin meaning "of the Adriatic" and "dark one."

ADWIN (ah-DWEEN) Akan of Ghana word meaning "artist" or "thinker."

AESOP (EE-sop, EE-suhp) This sixth century B.C. Greek fable writer was a former slave. He has been described as an Aethiopian (meaning African) with a hunchback.

AFEWORK (AH-fuh-wurk) Amharic of Ethiopia male name meaning "one who speaks only of pleasant things, one who does not speak of bad and evil things."

AFEWORKI (ah-fuh-wur-KEE) The Tigrinya of Ethiopia version of the name AFEWORK above.

AFRAM (ah-FRAHM) Akan of Ghana male name referring to the Afram River in Ghana's Ashanti Region. This important waterway is fifty-five miles (ninety kilometers) long and dries up from October to March. Afram is also used as a surname.

AFRICANUS (ah-free-KAHN-oos) This name was used in ancient Greco-Roman societies for men of African origin.

AHMADOU (AM-a-doo) West African male name. Ahmadou Kourouma was born in Cote D'Ivoire. His 1968 novel, *The Suns of Independence*, is a classic of African literature.

AKELLO (ah-KEHL-oh) Alur of Uganda male name meaning "I have brought" or "bring forth."

AKII-BUA (ah-kee-BOO-ah) John Akii-Bua won Uganda's first Olympic gold medal in 1972 for the 400-meter hurdles in a time of 47.82 seconds.

AKIN (ah-KEEN) Yoruba of Nigeria male name meaning "warrior, hero, brave man." This name is often used in combination with other names. Examples are **AKINWOLE** (ah-keen-WOH-lay), which means "bravery enters this home;" **AKINTUNDE** (ah-keen-TOON-day), meaning "bravery returns;" **AKINSANYA** (ah-keen-SAHN-yah), "bravery gets revenge"; and **AKINYEMI** (ah-keen-YAY-mee), meaning "fated to be a warrior."

ALADIAN   The Aladian are a people from Cote D'Ivoire who speak a Kwa language.

ALAFIN (ah-LAH-feen)   A title meaning "king" formerly used by the Yoruba people of Nigeria.

ALI (A-lee, AH-lee)   Swahili and Muslim male name meaning "noble, exalted." Ali Mazrui, born in Kenya, is a renowned scholar who wrote and presented the BBC television series "The Africans" and wrote a book of the same name.

ALPHA (AL-fah)   Guinean male name meaning "leader." Alpha Blondy is an African-style reggae singer from Cote D'Ivoire. Born in 1953 in the town of Dimbokoro, Blondy's real name is Seydou Kone.

AMADI (ah-MAH-dee)   a) Ibo of Nigeria name for both males and females. Amadi refers to a minor deity, the Sun God. Use of the name signifies dedication to Amadi and means "rejoice." b) Swahili male name. c) A town in southern Sudan.

AMAN (AH-mahn)   Amharic of Ethiopia male name heard mostly in Welo Province of northern Ethiopia. It means "peace" and is often used as a nickname.

AMANI (ah-MAH-nee)   A Kiswahili word meaning "peace."

AMARE (ah-MAHR-uh)   A male name in both Amharic and Tigrinya of Ethiopia which means "he is good looking."

AMAZU (ah-MAH-zoo)   Ibo of Nigeria male name meaning "no one knows everything."

ANDRIANAMPOINAIMERINA   (ahn-dree-ahn-nah-POO-ee-nee-MAIR-i-nah) Ruler of the Merina kingdom from 1787 until 1810 when he died. Known as **NAMPOINA**, he united and ruled the peoples and lands of the central plateau of Madagascar and constructed a magnificent hilltop palace. (Could be shortened to **ANDRIAN** or **ANDI**.)

ANTHONY (AN-thuh-nee)   a) Born near Memphis, Egypt, Antony, or Anthony (A.D. 251 to 356) was a hermit who organized the first Christian monastery. He is a Catholic saint whose feast day is January 17. b) Chief Anthony was a journalist and politician whose autobiography, *Fugitive Offender,* related his experiences while in prison for treason. He was born in Mid-Western State, Nigeria in 1923. c) Anthony is derived from Latin and means "inestimable."

ARABI (uh-RAHB-ee)   This Egyptian soldier led an army revolt against French and English imperialist forces in 1881. He was captured and jailed.

AREN (AHR-ehn)   Nigerian male name meaning "eagle." Also, a Scandinavian male name meaning "rule" or "eagle."

ARI (AH-ree)   The Ari people live in Cote D'Ivoire and speak a Kwa language. Also, Ari is a male name of Germanic origin meaning "eagle" and of Hebrew origin meaning "lion."

ASANTE (ah-SAHN-tay, uh-SAHN-tay)   A Kiswahili word for "thank you." b) Another name for the Ashanti people of Ghana. c) Asante is a well-known Ghanaian musician.

ASHUR (ah-SHOOR)   Swahili male name for a child born during the Muslim month of Ashur.

ASSEFA (ah-SUHF-ah)   Amharic of Ethiopia male name meaning "he has increased." The full meaning that is implied is "he has increased our family by coming into this world."

ATA (ah-TAH)   A popular name in Ghana for a male twin.

ATSU (ah-CHOO)   Ewe of Ghana name for a male twin.

AUGUSTINE (AW-guh-steen, aw-GUS-tin)   Saint Augustine was an important figure in early Christianity. He was called a Church Father, meaning he wrote down the laws of the church. Of Berber parentage, he was born in A.D. 354 in Algeria. Augustine studied in the ancient Roman city of Carthage (near present-day Tunis) and later became the Bishop of Hippone. His feast day is August 28. Augustine is a male name of Latin origin that means "venerable, exalted." Popular variants are **GUS, AUSTIN,** and **AUGUSTIN.**

AYUB (a-YIB)   Muslim male name meaning "penitent" and referring to the biblical Job. Ayub Kalule was a Ugandan professional boxer.

AYUBU (ah-YOOB-OO)   Swahili version of Ayub that means "patience in suffering."

AZENIA (ah-ZEEN-ee-uh)   King Azenia ruled the Agni people of west Africa in the sixteenth century A.D.

AZI (ah-ZEE)   Nigerian male name meaning "youth."

AZIZI (ah-ZEE-zee)   Swahili male name and Kiswahili word meaning "a treasure, excellent."

B

He who does not travel will not know
the value of men.

—Berber of North Africa proverb

Female

BAHATI (bah-HAH-tee) This Kiswahili word for "luck, fortune" is also a female name used in Swahili cultures.

BAHIMA (bah-HEE-mah) A people from Rwanda and Burundi, also referred to as the **BATUTSI** (bah-TOOT-see) or **TUTSI.** Traditionally the Bahima were nomadic cattle herders. Today, due to space constraints in the tiny countries in which they live, they mainly engage in farming on small plots.

BAKITA (bah-KEET-ah) Josefina Bakita was a nineteenth century Sudanese nun. She was sainted by Pope John Paul II in May, 1992.

BAKOKO (bah-KOH-koh) A people living in Cameroon who speak a Bantu language. (Could be **KOKO** for short.)

BALINDA (bah-LEEN-dah) A Rutooro of Uganda name meaning "patience, endurance, fortitude." (Although Balinda is used as a male name in Uganda, it is probably more suitable for females in English-language countries.)

BANNY (BAH-nee) The title and name of the main character of a song by West African musical group Toure Kunda. The song concerns a girl who leaves her village to find wealth in the city. Unsuccessful at this, she is embarrassed to return home. A village wiseman tells her that even if a person has nothing, they feel best at home.

BARA (BAH-rah)   a) A people living in southern Madagascar. b) A river in eastern Ethiopia. c) Bara or Bara Kuu (BAH-rah KOO) in Kiswahili means "continent, mainland." d) A female Hebrew name meaning "to choose."

BARAKA (bah-RAH-kah)   A Kiswahili word meaning "blessings, prosperity," and a Muslim word referring to the notion of "divine force or luck." Also, a Muslim female name meaning "blessing." This name is already popular among African Americans in some parts of the United States.

BASSA (BAH-sah)   Ethnic groups living in Liberia and eastern Cameroon as well as the name of their language. Spelled **BASA**, it is the name of a people of central Nigeria.

BATHSHEBA (bath-SHEE-buh)   Also known as **BATSHEVA**, this is the daughter of the Queen of Sheba, the legendary ruler of Abyssinia (modern-day Ethiopia). The name means "daughter of the oath."

BEIRA (BAY-ruh)   A port city in east central Mozambique and the capital of Sofala Province. Beira's rail connections to neighboring countries Malawi, Zimbabwe, Zambia, and Zaire make it an important, strategic port. The city's name comes from the Portuguese for "shore" and was named after Portugal's Beira Province.

BEJA (BAY-juh)   a) A nomadic, cattle- and camel-herding people of Sudan's Nubian Desert. They are of Egyptian and Arab ancestry, originating in Saudi Arabia and the Sinai Peninsula. They remain Orthodox Muslims and speak a Cushitic language. Beja women adorn themselves with gold jewelry as a sign of wealth. b) Beja (bay-ZHAH) is also a busy market town in northern Tunisia near Tunis, the capital.

BELA (BAY-lah)   A Kongo word meaning "to perch."

BELLA (BEHL-ah)   a) A people found in the west African savannah in Burkina Faso and Mali. Formerly, the Bella were slaves to the Tuareg. Bella is a Zerma word meaning both "slave" and "freed slave." b) (BEHL-uh)   An Italian female name that means "beautiful."

BENGUELA (behn-GWEHL-uh, behn-GEHL-uh)   A principal coast town in Angola. Also, the Benguela Current is a cold ocean current that flows from Cape Town up the west coast of Africa which has caused much of the southwest coast (Namibia) to become a desert. Benguela means "defence" in a local language.

BERENICE (behr-uh-NEE-kay, behr-uh-NEES, BEHR-uh-NIGH-see) The original name of Benghazi, a coastal town in Libya, which originated in the fifth century B.C. Also, the ruins of an ancient city in southeastern Egypt. Berenice is a Greek female name meaning "one who brings victory."

BERHANE (bur-HAH-nay) Female and male name in the Amharic and Tigrinya languages of Ethiopia which means "my light."

BERTA (BUR-tah) A people found in Sudan and Ethiopia. They speak a language shared by no other language group. Also, Berta is a short form of the Teutonic name Alberta that means "brilliant, illustrious."

BETA ISRAEL (BAY-tuh IZ-ree-uhl) The name used by Falashas, or Ethiopian Jews, for themselves. It translates as "House of Israel."

BE TAMMATITE The original name of the **TAMBERMA** people of northern Togo. It means "skilled at masonry" as they were known for their unique houses made of clay and wood.

BETI (BEH-tee) A people of Cameroon. Also, a Kiswahili word pronounced BAY-tee and meaning "verse of a song" or "small leather pouch."

BETSIBOKA (beht-si-BOOK-kah) At 325 miles (523 kilometers) this is the largest river in Madagascar, located in the country's northwest. (Could be shortened to **BETSI** or **BOKA**.)

BETSIMISARAKA (beht-si-mis-AHR-ah-kah) The name of a principal city as well as a people in the northeast region of Madagascar. The Betsimisaraka are the second largest ethnic group living on the east coast. Their main source of livelihood is fishing and farming of mainly coffee, cloves and vanilla. Their name means "inseparable people" or "many united." The original Empire of the Betsimisaraka was founded by

Ratsimilaho, who was born of a Malagasy mother and an English pirate father. (Could be shortened to **BETSI** with **MISARAKA** as a middle name.)

BIBI (BEE-bee)   a) An East African female name meaning "daughter of a king." b) A Kiswahili word meaning "lady" or "grandmother." Bibi is used in East Africa to refer to a man's girlfriend; "bibi yako" could be translated as "my woman" or "my lady."

BILMA (BIL-muh)   An oasis town in the Sahara Desert in northeast Niger. Salt reserves have put Bilma on the Sahara trade route maps for over five hundred years.

BINATA (bee-NAH-tah)   A popular Wolof of Senegal name for females.

BINTA (BEEN-tah)   West African female name meaning "with God."

BONNY (BAHN-ee)   A coastal city in southeastern Nigeria at the mouth of the Bonny River. Also, a female name of Latin origin meaning "pretty."

BRAVA (BRAHV-uh)   a) On the Indian Ocean coast in Somalia, this town is a main port for dhows—Swahili and Arab old-style sailboats that plow the coast of East Africa and the Indian Ocean. b) One of the southern Cape Verde islands.

BRIA (bree-AH)   A city in eastern Central African Republic located on the Kotto River.

BUCHI (BOO-chee)   Buchi Emecheta is a Nigerian writer. Her works include *The Rape of Shavi* and *Second-Class Citizen.*

BUPE (BOO-peh)   A Nyakyusa of Tanzania female name meaning "hospitality."

BUSIA (boo-SEE-uh)   A city in Western Province Kenya, mainly populated by Luya peoples. Also, an African surname. Dr. Kofi Abrefa Busia was Prime Minister of Ghana from 1969–1972 as well as a renowned author.

BWEJUU (bWAY-JOO)   A village and beach on the Indian Ocean coast of Tanzania's Zanzibar island. This unspoilt coastal region has palm forests and world-class coral reefs. With new guest houses and beachfront hotels in the works, Bwejuu will certainly become more popular with tourists.

BABA (BAH-bah)   In the Kiswahili language of East Africa and in Fulani, Yoruba, and various other West African languages this word means "father" or "elder."

BABATUNDE (bah-bah-TOON-day)   Yoruba of Nigeria male name defined as "father has returned" which means the child resembles one of his grandfathers. The popular short form of this name is **TUNDE**

BABU (BAH-boo)   A Kiswahili word and male name meaning "grandfather." Also, a West African male name meaning "willing."

BABUKAR (bab-oo-KAHR)   This male name is popular among the Wolof of Senegal.

BADRU (BAH-droo)   Swahili male name meaning "born at full moon." It is a variation of the Arabic name **BADR AL DIN** (bahdr-ahl-DEEN) which means "full moon of faith." (Could be shortened to **DRU**.)

BADU (bah-DOO)   An Ashanti of Ghana name for tenth-born children.

BANGUI (bahng-GEE)   The capital of the Central African Republic. The name means "the rapids" in a local language.

BANJUL (BAHN-jool)   The capital and largest city of The Gambia. Banjul was founded in 1816 by the British, who used it as a base for suppressing the slave trade. The city is built on the island of St. Mary near the mouth of the Gambia River. Its name is believed to mean "rope mats."

BARCE (BAHR-chay)   Also known as **BARKA** or **BARCA** (BAHR-kuh), these are the ruins of an ancient Greek town in northern Libya found near the city of Benghazi. Barce was founded in the sixth century B.C. and destroyed some 300 years later.

BARRY (BAHR-ee)   A Guinean surname denoting that the family comes from the Peul, Fulani, or Foulbe ethnic groups of West Africa. Barry is also a modern English male name with various significances: "ruler of the home"; of the Barry Islands in Wales; or, "good marksman."

BASEL (BAS-il)   Muslim male name meaning "brave" that is popular in the Sudan.

BASSEY (BAH-see)   Efik of Nigeria unisex name of uncertain origin and meaning.

BATIAN   This peak of Mount Kenya is 17,058 feet (5,199 meters) high. It was named after a Masai chief.

BAYI   Filbert Bayi was born in Arusha, Tanzania, at the foot of Mt. Kilimanjaro. In 1957 in Kingston, Jamaica, he set the world record for running the mile with a time of 3:51. He held the title for the 1,500-meter run from 1974–1979.

BEKELE (buh-KUH-luh)   Amharic of Ethiopia male name meaning "he has grown, he has come into being."

BELUCHI (bay-LOOCH-ee)   Ibo people of Nigeria male name meaning "provided God approves."

BEN AISSA (behn-AY-suh)   A town in Tunisia. Ben is a Hebrew name meaning "son" and Aissa is a Muslim name meaning "Jesus."

BENDEL (BEHN-dl, behn-DEHL)   A state in southern Nigeria, formerly called Mid-Western State.

BENGHAZI (behn-GAHZ-ee)   Also spelled **BENGASI,** this is a city in northeast Libya on the Mediterranean Sea. Originally a Greek settlement, today it is Libya's main seaport and sister capital to Tripoli. The city earned its name from the Muslim saint, Ben-Ghazi, whose grave is nearby.

BENI (BAY-nee)   A town in northern Zaire near the Ugandan border and the foot of the Ruwenzori Mountains.

BENI ABBES (BEHN-nee ah-BEHS)   A beautiful oasis town in Algeria in the Grand Erg Occidental region of the Sahara Desert.

BENI AMER (BEHN-nee ah-MAIR)   A people belonging to the Beja ethnic group (see BEJA) who live in the Nubian Desert of northern Sudan.

BENI HASSAN (BEHN-ee HA-san)   A town on the east banks of the Nile River in Egypt. It is the site of the Hatshepsut Temple and thirty-nine rock-hewn tombs of ancient royalty, dating from around 2,000 B.C.   The name means "children of Hassan" in Arabic.

BERHANU (bur-HAH-noo)   Amharic of Ethiopia male name meaning "his light."

BERIHUN (bair-EE-hoon)   Amharic and Tigrinya of Ethiopia male name meaning "let him be our gate/our guidance."

BERTA (BUR-tah)   Amharic of Ethiopia male name meaning "be strong, be vigilant, persevere." This name is commonly used among the Gurage people of central Ethiopia.

BIKO (BEE-koh)   Steven Biko was a South African political activist who was instrumental in starting the Black Consciousness movement in 1969. He died while in police custody on September 12, 1977.

BILAL (bee-LAHL)   A Muslim male name which is popular in North Africa. It means "black man" and refers to Muhammed's first convert.

BISSAU (bi-SOW)   The capital city of Guinea-Bissau. It was named after a chief of the Bissau people who inhabit the island on which the city is found. Bissau was established in 1692 and became the country's capital in 1942.

BIWOT (BEE-wot)   Amos Biwott is the Kenyan athlete who won an Olympic gold medal in 1968 for the 3,000-meter Steeplechase in a time of 8:51.0.

BO (boh)   a) A people of Burkina Faso. b) The local name of a West African tree, the bark of which is used to make a traditional diuretic medicine. c) The second largest city in Sierra Leone and the capital of Bo District. d) A Danish male name meaning "commanding," and a female Chinese name meaning "precious."

BOBO (boh-BOH)   a) Fante of Ghana name for males born on Tuesday. b) Ewe of West Africa male name meaning "be humble." c) A people living in Mali and Burkina Faso who speak dialects of Gur. d) Bobo Dioulasso (BOH-boh dyoo-LAS-oh), commonly referred to as just Bobo, is the second largest city in Burkina Faso.

BOESAK (BOH-sak)   Reverend Allan Aubrey Boesak of the Dutch Reformed Church of South Africa is a leader of the Christian anti-apartheid sentiment. In 1982, he became

President of the World Alliance of Reformed Churches, which represents Protestants worldwide.

BOKHARI (book-HAHR-ee) A Malian male name.

BOLAJI (boh-LAH-jee) Yoruba of Nigeria male name.

BRISTOL (BRIS-t'l) King Bristol was a paramount chief of the Bassa people of Liberia, who in the 1800s took black American colonizers hostage.

BURKINA FASO (bur-KEEN-uh fah-SOH) In 1984, President Thomas Sankara changed the name of this West African country from the European name of Upper Volta to Burkina Faso, which means "land of the honest people." (Could be shortened to **BURK.**)

BUSIRIS (byoo-SIGH-ruhs) An ancient Egyptian king who had the unpleasant habit of killing visitors to his city. Also, an ancient Egyptian city that was the center for worship of Osiris, the god of nature. The name Busiris means "Temple of Osiris."

BUTHELEZI (boo-teh-LAY-zee) Gatsha Buthelezi, a Zulu chief, is an outspoken proponent of a non-racial South Africa. (Could be shortened to **BUTH.**)

BUTROS (BOO-trohs) Also spelled **BOUTROS**, this is a Muslim male name referring to the biblical Peter. In 1992, Boutros Boutros-Ghali became the first diplomat from the continent of Africa to fill the post of United Nations Secretary-General. Ghali is an Egyptian who has been Professor of International Law at Cairo University and Deputy Prime Minister of Egypt.

BWANA (BWAH-nah) Also **MBWANA** (m-BWAH-nah), this Kiswahili word and Swahili male name means "gentleman, mister, sir."

C

The Birth of Shaka (Chaka)

His baby cry
was of a cub
tearing the neck
of the lioness
because he was fatherless.

The gods
boiled his blood
in a clay pot of passion
to course in his veins.

His heart was shaped into an ox shield
to foil every foe.

Ancestors forged
his muscles into
thongs as tough
as wattle bark
and nerves
as sharp as
syringa thorns.

His eyes were lanterns
that shone from the dark valleys of Zululand
to see white swallows
coming across the sea.
His cry to two assassin brothers:
"Lo, you can kill me
but you'll never rule this land!"
> —From *Sounds of a Cowhide Drum*, by Mbuyiseni
> Oswald Mtshali, a South African poet

24

Female

CABINDA (kuh-BIN-duh)   This is a small, noncontiguous enclave of Angola sandwiched between the Congo and Zaire on the Atlantic coast. Its off-shore oil fields have attracted oil companies since the 1960s.

CANDACE (kan-DAHK-ay, KAN-duh-see, kan-DAY-see)   Also spelled **KANDAKE** or **KENTAKE,** this was the title used for queens of the ancient Nubian Kingdom of Kush (now northern Sudan). It is a royal title meaning "queen mother" and was similar in use to the title Pharaoh used by ancient Egypt's kings. The first known Candace was admired for her exceptional beauty as well as her fierce resistance to Roman invaders led by Augustus Caesar. She lost an eye leading her troops into the battle.

CARMONA (kahr-MOH-nah)   A town in northern Angola.

CASSIOPEA (ka-see-oh-PEE-uh)   In Greek mythology, beautiful Cassiopea was mother of Andromeda and wife of the Aethiopian (meaning black African) king Cepheus. Her name means "cassia juice."

CHANYA (CHAHN-yuh)   A Taita people of Kenya female name.

CHARA (CHAHR-ah)   A people living in southwest Ethiopia. They speak a language from the Ometo language group.

CHARICLEA (kair-i-KLEE-uh)   In his novel *Aethiopica,* the ancient Roman writer Heliodorus created a fictional female character who has two black African parents (then referred to as Aethiopians), but is born with white skin and golden hair. (Could be shortened to **CHARI** or **CLEA.**)

CHERANGANI (chair-ahn-GAH-nee)   The Cherangani Hills in Kenya are home of the Pokot people. With heights of up to 10,000 feet (3,030 meters), the hills are popular with trekkers. (Could be shortened to **CHERI.**)

CHICHA (CHEE-chah)   A Kiswahili word meaning "grated coconut."

CHIKU (CHEE-koo)   A Swahili female name meaning "chatterer."

CHINA (CHEE-nah) A Shona of Zimbabwe word for "Thursday."

CHINAKA (chee-NAH-kah) An Ibo of Nigeria female name meaning "God decides."

CHINARA (chee-NAHR-ah) An Ibo of Nigeria female name meaning "may God receive."

CHIONE (KEE-oh-nee, KIGH-oh-nee) This Greek mythological figure bore a son by Poseidon named Eumolpus. Chione tossed Eumolpus into the sea but he was rescued by his father, Poseidon, and later washed ashore on the Aethiopian coast. The Greek word chione means "snow," and the name means "snow maiden."

CIRCE (SIR-see) According to Greek mythology, this African witch transformed the Greek troops of Odysseus into swine. The classical Greek pronunciation of her name is KEAR-kay.

CLEOPATRA (KLEE-uh-PA-truh) Called "the Queen of Kings," Cleopatra VII reigned as Queen of Egypt from 51–30 B.C. She was born in 69 B.C. in Alexandria, Egypt and is believed to have been black African. Cleopatra supported Marcus Antonius against Octavius in the Roman Civil War. Antonius was defeated and Egypt was conquered by Octavius. The turn of events led Cleopatra to commit suicide by snakebite in 30 B.C. The name Cleopatra means "famous." (This name can be shortened to **CLEA**.)

COCO (KOH-koh) Coco Beach is on the Atlantic Ocean in northern Gabon.

COCODY (koh-koh-DEE) A residential section of Abidjan, the capital city of Cote D'Ivoire. The University of Abidjan is located here. Alpha Blondy, a reggae singer from Cote D'Ivoire, released a hit song called "Cocody Rock."

CONSTANTINE (KON-stuhn-teen) A large city in northeastern Algeria situated atop a rock plateau overlooking the canyons of the Rhummel River. It was once the ancient Roman city of Cirta. The city was renamed in the fourth century A.D. by the Turkish ruler who also gave his name to Constantinople, Turkey (now Istanbul). Constantine is also a female name of Latin origin meaning "constant, faithful, firm."

CRISPINA (kris-PEEN-uh, kris-PIN-uh)   A female name meaning "curly haired." Born in Thagara, Africa, Crispina was persecuted for her Christian faith. She is a Catholic saint whose feast day is December 5.

Male

CAESARIUS (kigh-ZAHR-ee-uhs)   A legendary African deacon who was killed for protesting the sacrifice of youths to the gods. He is a Catholic saint whose feast day is November 1. (Could be shortened to **CAESAR**, pronounced SEE-zuhr.)

CAMARA (kah-mah-rah)   A West African male name meaning "teacher." Also, it is a Guinean surname indicating the family belongs to the Mandinka or Soussou tribe. Camara Laye (1928–1980) is a writer from Guinea whose books, written in French, include *Dark Child* and *The Radiance of the King*.

CAMEROON (kam-eh-ROON)   Also spelled **CAMEROUN**, this country on the Gulf of Guinea has a surface area of 183,381 square miles (469,455 kilometers), making it larger than the state of California. Its name is derived from the Portuguese word "camarao," meaning "shrimp" (the shellfish), due to the abundance of shrimp in the gulf waters. Mount Cameroon has an elevation of 13,353 feet (4,072 meters), making it the highest point in western Africa south of the Sahara.

CARNOT (kahr-NOH)   A town in southwestern Central African Republic.

CEPHEUS (KEHF-ee-uhs, SEH-fee-uhs, SEE-fee-uhs, SEE-fyoos)   According to Greek legend, this Aethiopian (meaning black African) king was husband of Cassiopea and father of Andromeda. (Could be shortened to **CEPH**.)

CESS (sehs)   Also known as the **CESTOS** (SEHS-tuhs), this river is in Liberia. The Cess is two hundred miles (320 kilometers) long and it empties into the Atlantic Ocean at River Cess Town.

CHAD (chad) a) The fifth largest country in Africa. With a surface area of 495,752 square miles (1,284,000 square kilometers) it is twice the size of Texas. The official language is French. Half of Chad's population are Muslims; the other half practice local traditional religions or Christianity. The country adopted its name from Lake Chad which is believed to be derived from a local word meaning "huge expanse of water." b) Lake Chad, fed by the Chari River, is in southern Chad. Surrounded by marshes the lake can cover up to ten thousand square miles (25,600 square kilometers), but can also be half that size due to seasonal changes. Natron, or sodium bicarbonate, is mined around the lake. c) A Celtic male name that means "battle" or "warlike."

CHAGA (CHAH-gah) Also spelled **CHAGGA** or **SHAGA** these Tanzanian people live mainly in the Kilimanjaro region and speak a Bantu language. The Kiswahili word "chaga" means "to do vigorously" and "be prevalent."

CHAKA (CHAH-kah, SHAH-kah) Also spelled **SHAKA**, a South African male name meaning "Great King." Chaka was a Zulu king (1800–1828) and military strategist who founded the Zulu nation. The son of a Nguni chief, Chaka was born in 1773 and was assassinated in 1828.

CHALBI (CHAHL-bee) Also spelled **CHELBI**, the Chalbi Desert is located east of Lake Turkana in northern Kenya. It is home to the Gabbra people.

CHANGA (CHAHN-gah) In the seventeenth century, this warrior chief conquered the Monomotapa kingdom in present-day Mozambique and Zimbabwe, and also attacked Portuguese strongholds in the area. He fancied calling himself **CHANGAMIRE** (chahn-gah-MEER-ay), having attached the Arabic title of Amir to his name.

CHEGE (CHEH-gay) A Kikuyu people of Kenya male name.

CHEIKH (shayk) Guinean male name meaning "learned." Cheikh Hamidou Kane is a Senegalese politician and writer whose novel *Ambiguous Adventure* won the 1962 Grand Prix Litteraire de l'Afrique Noir.

CHEKE (CHEE-kay) A people living in Nigeria and Cameroon who speak a language from the Bata language group.

CHEOPS (KEE-ops) A pharaoh of Egypt's IV dynasty (2900–2875 B.C.) He is famous for having built Egypt's largest pyramid, the Great Pyramid at Giza. Cheops was believed to have had negroid facial features. He was known as Cheops to the ancient Greeks, but was called **KHUFU** by the Egyptians.

CHEPHREN (KEHF-rehn) The Greek name of the son of Cheops. Chephren built Egypt's second largest pyramid and the Sphinx at Giza. His Egyptian name is **KHAFRA**.

CHICHA (CHEE-chah) A West African male name meaning "beloved." It is also a Kiswahili word meaning "grated coconut."

CHIMELA (chee-MEHL-ah) Chimela "Chimel" Anaba is a Nigerian fashion designer based in London. Although born of Nigerian parents, he was raised and educated primarily in England. Chimel has made fashions for the rich and famous, including the Princess of Wales.

CHINUA (CHEEN-oo-ah) Ibo of Nigeria male name meaning "God's own blessing" or "may God hear." Chinua Achebe is a preeminent Nigerian writer and poet. His novels include *Girls at War* (1972), *Man of the People* (1966), *No Longer at Ease* (1960), and *Things Fall Apart* (1958).

CHIROMO (chee-ROH-moh) A town in southern Malawi.

CONAKRY (KON-uh-kree) Also spelled **KONAKRI**, this port city is the capital of Guinea. Conakry is built on the island of Tombo. It is the center of the bauxite industry.

COTONOU (koh-ton-OO, koh-toh-NOO) The largest city in Benin, Contonou is a seaport and an industrial and commercial center. It was established in 1851 on the Gulf of Guinea.

CYPRIAN ((SIP-ree-uhn, KIP-ree-uhn) A male name of Latin origin meaning "native of Cyprus." a) Cyprian (A.D. 200–

258) served as bishop of the Roman city-state of Carthage (present-day Tunisia). This Catholic saint was born with the name Thascius Caecilius Cyprianus. b) Cyprian Ekwensi is a Nigerian novelist whose works include *Survive the Peace, Burning Grass, Jagua Nana, People of the City,* and *Lokotown.* Ekwensi was born in 1921 in Minna, northern Nigeria.

D

O, the good times of marriage
When adults chat over small things
And the woman holds her man
And says, "Father of so and so."
Then I answer, "Yes, yes."
I answer as I put my spears away;
I put my spears away after a journey,
Aker, I do so without words.
    —Dinka of South Sudan song about marriage, from
             Francis M. Deng's *The Dinka of the Sudan*

Female

DADA (DAH-dah)   a) Kiswahili word for "sister." b) Yoruba of Nigeria female name for children with curly hair. c) West African deity of nature.

DALILA (dah-LEE-lah)   Also spelled **DALIA** (dah-LEE-ah), this Swahili female name means "gentle."

DAURA (DOR-uh)   Hausa legend tells of Queen Daura, a priestess-chief who married Bayajida. Daura is the name of the city in northern Nigeria where these legends are fostered.

DE (day)   Also called **DEWOI** (deh-WOH) or **DO**, these people of northern Liberia speak a dialect of Kru.

DEBA (DAY-buh)   A large town in North-Eastern State, Nigeria.

DEBBA (DEHB-uh)   Also known as **ED DEBBA** and **AD DABBAH** (ad-DAB-uh). A town in northern Sudan on the Nile River.

DEBRE (DEH-bruh)   This Ethiopian word means "mount" as in mountain or hill.

DEBRE BERHAN (DEH-bruh bur-HAHN)   Under the rule of Emperor Zere Iacob, this was the capital of the Zagwe dynasty of Ethiopia around the thirteenth century.

DEBRE DAMO (DEH-bruh DAH-moh)   A historic monastery in Ethiopia.

DEBRE MARKOS (DEH-bruh MAHR-kohs)   The capital city of the Gojam Region in western Ethiopia. The city's population is over 45,000.

DEBRE TABOR (DEH-bruh TAH-bohr)   A highland town near Lake Tana in western Ethiopia.

DEBRE ZEIT (DEH-bruh ZAYT)   This city is found in the Shewa Region of central Ethiopia and has a population over 57,000.

DEBTERA (duhb-TUH-rah)   An Amharic of Ethiopia word for a priest who is in training.

DEKA (DEH-kah)   Somali female name meaning "one who pleases."

DELA EDEN (deh-LAH AY-dehm)   Ewe of West Africa male and female name meaning "savior."

DELA O KANDE (day-LAH oh KAHN-day)   Nigerian name for a female born after many males.

DENDERAH (DEHN-duh-rah)   Also spelled **DENDERA**, this village on the Nile River in Egypt is the site of an ancient temple dedicated to Hathor, a goddess represented by a female head with cow ears. The temple was completed in 60 A.D. The Egyptian god Isis is said to have come from Denderah.

DESSIE (DEHS-see-ay)   Also called **DESE** (DAY-say) and **DESSE** (DEHS-say). A large town located enroute from Addis Ababa to Asmara in Eritrea (contested province of northern Ethiopia). It is the capital of Welo Province and abuts the Great Rift Valley. Dessie is an important trading center for grains, honey, hides and beeswax.

DESTA (DUH-stah)   Amharic of Ethiopia female and male name meaning "joy, happiness."

DIANI (dee-AH-nee)   Diani Beach is found south of Mombasa on Kenya's Indian Ocean coast. The white-sand beach stretching six miles (ten kilometers) and fringed with palm trees makes it popular with tourists.

DIDESSA (di-DUH-sah)   An Oromo name for a river in Ethiopia that is a tributary of the Blue Nile. (Could be shortened to **DI** or **DESSA**.)

DIDYME (DID-uh-muh)   An ancient Greco-Roman writer, Asclepiades, praised Didyme, a woman of African origin, for her beauty.

DILLA (DIL-lah)   A town in southern Ethiopia.

DILOLO (di-LOH-loh)   The name of a lake in eastern Angola and a town across the border in Zaire. The lake is the subject of local legend (see the name MOENA) and its name is believed to mean "despair." (Could be shortened to **DI** or **LOLO**.)

DIMI (DEE-mee)   Dimi Mint Abba is a singer from Mauritius whose album is called "Moorish Music from Mauritania" (World Circuit label).

DJANET (JAN-eht)   An oasis town in southern Algeria in the Sahara Desert which has for centuries been a stopping point for trans-Saharan caravans.

DJEMILA (juh-MEE-luh)   The Arabic name for the ruins of the ancient Roman market town Ciucul, located near the modern town of Setif in the Atlas Mountains of northern Algeria. Ciucul was founded in the first century A.D. as a Roman military and administrative colony. Djemila is an Arabic word meaning "beautiful."

DJENNE (jeh-NAY)   Also spelled **JENNE**, this town was founded around the eighth century A.D. It is located about three hundred miles (480 kilometers) southwest of Timbuktu on a branch of the Niger River in the Mopti Region of central Mali. The town is constructed of mud-bricks, as is the twelfth century Mosque made in Sudanese architectural style for which it is famous. Djenne is referred to as "the jewel of the Niger" and "the Venice of the Sudan." Old Djenne, now abandoned, was an important center of Islamic culture and learning in the Kingdom of Mali.

DJIDADE (jee-DAHD-ay)   Fulani of West Africa name for both males and females meaning "desired."

DJOUDJ (jooj)   This Senegalese national park is located along the border with Mauritania and is an important reserve for wild pigs and ducks.

DOLIE (doh-LIGH)   A popular Somali female name.

DORI (DOH-ree)   a) A town in the Sahel, the southern edge of the Sahara Desert, in northern Burkina Faso. b) Dori is also a short form of the female name Adora, which is of Latin origin and means "beloved."

DORLETA (dor-LAY-tah)   Zimbabwean female name referring to the biblical Mary.

DUMA (DOO-mah)   These are a people living in Gabon. Another people with the same name are found in Zimbabwe. Both speak a Bantu-based language.

DYAN a) (DEE-an)   A people of Burkina Faso that speak a dialect of Lobi. b) (digh-AN)   Dyan is also a form of the female name Diana, which is of Latin origin meaning "bright" and refers to Diana the goddess of the moon according to Roman mythology.

Male

DABIR (dah-BEER, DAB-ir)   Muslim male name popular in North Africa, mainly in Egypt and Algeria, that means "teacher, secretary."

DAG (dahg)   A seventeenth-century West African prince who had his stomach torn open by one of his own attendants.

DAHOMEY (duh-HOH-mee)   Former name of Benin and name of a seventeenth to nineteenth century kingdom in the same region. According to legend, a local king named Da was killed by his rival who then built a city over Da's dismembered body. Thus Dahomey means "on the belly of Da."

DAKAR (dak-ahr, duh-KAHR)   The capital city of Senegal and a major west African harbor. Founded in 1857, Dakar sits on the south side of Cape Verde Peninsula. The city's name is believed to come from a Wolof word meaning "tamarind tree."

DALMAR (DAHL-mahr)   Somali male name that means "versatile."

DAN (dan)   a) An ethnic group from northeast Namibia, also called the **DAMARA, DAMAQUE** and **BERGDAMA**. They speak Nama, a Hottentot language. b) An agricultural people of west Africa, mainly in southern Cote D'Ivoire, of the Mandinka ethnic group. Traditionally the Dan live in forested areas and carve beautiful ceremonial wooden masks. c) Some scholars contend that Falashas (Ethiopian Jews) are descendants of one of the twelve tribes of Israel, the Dan tribe. d) In modern English usage Dan means "he judged." In the Bible, Dan is one of the twelve sons of Jacob.

DANAKIL (DUH-nah-keel, DAN-uh-kil)   Also called **AFAR** (AH-fahr) and **ADAL** (AH-dahl), these people live mainly in the Danakil Depression, a desert in northern Ethiopia and Djibouti. They are nomadic herders who speak Afar, a Cushitic language.

DANIACHEW (dahn-YAH-choh)   Amharic of Ethiopia male name meaning "you be their judge, arbitrate between them."

DANSO (DAN-soh)   Ashanti of Ghana male name meaning "reliable."

DAR (dahr)   a) Dar Es Salaam (dhar ehs suh-LAHM), often referred to simply as Dar, is Tanzania's principal city and former capital. Located on the Indian Ocean, the city's name comes from Arabic and means "haven of peace." b) Dar is also a Hebrew name meaning "mother of pearl."

DAREN (DAH-rehn)   Hausa of West Africa male name meaning "born at night." The modern English names Darren or Darin mean "small great one" or "wealthy."

DAUDI (dah-oo-dee)   Also spelled **DAUDY**, this Swahili male name meaning "beloved" is a version of the Arabic name **DAWUD** (dah-OOD) and refers to the biblical David. The ruler of the West African Songhai Empire from A.D. 1549–1582 was named Askia (king) Dawud.

DAVIE (dah-vee-ay) A town in Togo known for its unique style of cemetery headstones.

DAWIT (DAH-weet) Ethiopian male name referring to the biblical David. David is the Hebrew name meaning "beloved."

DELPHOS (DEHL-fos) Also spelled **DELPHUS** (DEHL-fus). The mythological founder of the town of Delphi in ancient Greece, who some believe is Aethiopian (meaning black African). His parentage is unclear; he is either the son of Poseidon and Melantho, or Apollo and Melanis.

DEMISSIE (duh-MUH-say) Amharic of Ethiopia male name meaning "destroyer."

DIA (DEE-ah, DEE-uh) a) A West African male name meaning "champion." b) A seventh-century dynasty whose kingdom was located around northwestern modern Nigeria. c) A Kiswahili word meaning "ransom, compensation."

DIARA (dee-AHR-ah) Male name of French-speaking West Africa that means "gift."

DIJI (DEE-jee) Ibo of Nigeria male name meaning "farmer."

DIN (deen) Congolese male name meaning "great."

DINIZULU (deen-ee-ZOO-loo) The son of King Cetshwayo, Dinizulu became ruler of the Zulus in 1884. He led the unsuccessful Zulu rebellion of 1906, a struggle for a united and independent Zululand. He died in 1913.

DOBI (DOH-bee) Kiswahili word meaning "a person who does laundry."

DODOMA (doh-DOH-mah) A city in central Tanzania constructed to be the new capital of Tanzania, replacing Dar Es Salaam.

DOMEVLO (doh-MEHV-loh) Ewe of Ghana male name meaning "don't take others for face value." (Could be shortened to **DOM**, itself a common short form of the Latin name DOMINIC, which means "of the Lord.")

DON a) An early African kingdom. b) Don Mattera is a South African poet and writer. c) Don is also an Irish male name meaning "ruler" or "chief."

DZIGBODE (gee-BOH-day) An Ewe of Ghana name meaning "patience."

E

When a snake is in the house, one need not discuss the matter at length.

—Ewe proverb

Female

EBRIE (eh-bree-AY) A people of Cote D'Ivoire who are known as "lagoon people." The Ebrie Lagoon, around which the city of Abidjan is built, boasts a residential and tourist area known as the "African Riviera."

EBIERE (ay-bee-AIR-ay, ee-bee-AIR-ay) Ijaw of Niger female name.

EFE (AYF-ay) Pygmies who live among the Balese tribe in the Ituri Forest of northeast Zaire and their language. The Efe, whose population is small, are cousins to the Mbuti and Batwa pygmies.

EFFIWAT (EHF-ee-wah) Nigerian female name of unknown origin.

EFIA (eh-FEE-ah) Fante of Ghana name for females born on Friday.

EFRA (eh-FRAH) A popular female name in Egypt.

ELAVAGNON (ay-lah-VAH-nyohn) A village in southern Togo whose name means "it will be alright, it will be well again." (Could be shortened to **ELA** or **AVA**.)

ELDELA (ehl-DEHL-ah) A village in the Garissa District in eastern Kenya near the town of Garbatula.

ELIMA (ay-LEEM-ah)   A separate religious organization for women of the Mbuti pygmies who live in the Ituri Forest of northeast Zaire.

ELMINA (ehl-MEE-nah)   A government-run rest house on the coast of Ghana that was originally a Portuguese-built fort in 1482 and later became a Dutch fort. Elmina means "the mine," as derived from Portuguese.

EOS (EE-os)   See AURORA.

ERINMWINDE (eh-rin-MWIN-day)   The beautiful wife of Oranmiyan, a twelfth-century ruler of the Benin Empire. (Could be shortened to **ERIN** or **MWINDE**.)

ESHE (AY-shay)   Swahili female name meaning "life."

ESHIRA (ay-SHEER-ah)   An ethnic group of Gabon that comprises about one-quarter of the country's population.

ESI (AY-see)   Ewe and Fante of Ghana name for females born on Sunday. Esi is one of the most common female names in Ghana.

ESIANKIKI   A Masai of Kenya and Tanzania word meaning "young maiden." (Could be shortened to **ESIAN** or **KIKI**.)

ESINAM (AY-see-nahm)   Ewe of Ghana female name meaning "God heard me."

ESNA (EHS-nuh)   Also called **ISNA** (IS-nuh), this town in southern Egypt is located along the west bank of the Nile River near the town of Luxor. Esna is the site of the ancient Temple of Khnum, a mythological Egyptian god who is depicted creating human beings on a potter's wheel.

ETOSHA (i-TOH-shuh)   Etosha National Park in northern Namibia is one of Africa's finest safari parks. The Etosha Pan is found in the middle of the Etosha National Park. This is a salt pan (a natural basin) 3,400 feet (1,000 meters) above sea level. Measuring 2,300 square miles (5,888 square kilometers), it is the largest salt pan in Africa.

EUTYCHIA (ay-yoo-TOO-kee-uh, yoo-TIK-ee-uh)   Also known as **ATALOUS**, this twelve-year-old black girl slave lived in the sixth century A.D. The name means "good luck" in Greek.

EVA (AY-vuh)   A Khoikhoi (Hottentot) woman of South Africa's Cape area who married a Dutch explorer named van Meerhoff in 1664, paving the way for societal acceptance of mixed European-African marriages at the time. Eva is a version of the name Eve, which comes from Hebrew and means "life."

EVALA (ay-VAH-lah)   Evala is the name of the Kabie people of Togo coming-of-age ceremony held for boys each July.

Male

EDET (ay-DEHT)   Ibibio and Efik peoples of Nigeria name for males born on market day, which is referred to as Edet.

EDO-BINI (eh-DOH-bee-NEE)   A former West African kingdom whose empire included modern Benin and parts of Nigeria. It is from this kingdom that the country of Benin derived its name.

EFFIOM (EHF-ee-om)   Efik of Nigeria male name meaning "crocodile."

ELESBAAN (ehl-ehs-BAHN)   A sixth-century king of the Axum Empire (present day northern Ethiopia). His troops ousted a Jewish king in Arabia who had been persecuting Christians. Elesbaan is a Catholic saint whose feast day is October 24.

ELGON (EHL-gon)   Mount Elgon is an extinct volcanic peak located on the border of Kenya and Uganda, northeast of Lake Victoria. Mount Elgon measures 14,176 feet (4,320 meters) high. Mount Elgon National Park is a pristine reserve covered by mountain, forest and bamboo jungle.

ELIMU (ay-LEE-moo)   A Kiswahili word meaning "science, knowledge."

EPHRAM (AY-frahm)   Europeanized variation of EFFIOM (see above).

ERASTO (eh-RAHS-toh)   An East African male name meaning "man of peace."

ERMIAS (AIR-mee-yahs)   Ethiopian male name referring to the biblical Jeremiah.

ESSIEN (ay-SHAN)   Ochi and Ga of Ghana name for sixth-born sons. Also, Ibibio and Efik of Nigeria name meaning "a child belongs to everyone."

EVIAN (eh-vee-AHN)   A twelfth-century king of the Benin Empire.

EZANA (ay-ZAHN-ah)   King Ezana of the Kingdom of Axum (now northern Ethiopia) adopted Christianity in the fourth century A.D. thus laying the groundwork for the development of Ethiopia's indigenous Christian faith.

EZEJI (ay-ZEH-jee, ee-ZEH-jee)   Ibo of Nigeria male name meaning "the king of yams" and symbolizing an elevated status among the community because of the family's bountiful stock of yams.

F

Of the distant past
I hear that horses used to fly,
In the world of today
horses no longer fly;
The land is full of sin
Yes, Miyom, ox of my father, sin is grave.
Of the distant past
I hear that Chief Kwol d'Arob de Biong
Charmed the crested cranes until he caught them;
In the world of today
No one can charm the crested cranes until he catches
them;
The land is full of sin
Yes, Miyom, my father's ox, sin is grave.
Even if people pray night and day
No one has the power of spirit
Unless we wake our ancestors from their graves.
—Song of the Dinka of South Sudan, from
Francis M. Deng's, *The Dinka of the Sudan*

Female

FALASHA (fuh-LAHSH-uh)   An Amharic word meaning "landless one," "immigrant," "outcast," or "stranger." The Falasha are a Jewish people of Ethiopia, most of whom have recently been airlifted to Israel.
FALASHINA (fah-lah-SHEEN-ah)   This is the Amharic word for the Cushitic language spoken by Falashas of Ethiopia.

41

FANA (FAH-nah)   a) Amharic and Tigrinya of Ethiopia female name meaning "light." b) A West African word meaning "jungle."

FANTA (FAHN-tah)   A female name from Guinea and Cote D'Ivoire meaning "beautiful day."

FANYA (FAHN-yah)   a) A very small ethnic group in Chad who speak Bua language. b) A Kiswahili word meaning "make" or "do." c) A Russian female name, short for **FAYINA**, meaning "free one."

FARA (FAHR-rah)   A Kiswahili word meaning "level measure." Spelled **FARAH** (FAIR-uh), it is a Muslim and Persian female name meaning "happiness, joy." Nuruddin Farah is a Somali writer (male) who wrote the novel *Maps*.

FARAS (FAHR-uhs)   Site on the Nile River in Sudan that was the former center of the Christian Kingdom of Nobatia. Faras is noted for its eighth to twelfth century frescoes.

FARIDA (fah-REE-dah)   Also spelled **FARIDAH**, Muslim female name meaning "precious pearl, only one, unique." Farida Karodia is a South African writer of Indian descent whose book, *Daughters of Twilight*, explores the plight of Asians and Coloreds under South Africa's apartheid system. She now lives in Canada.

FATIMA (FAT-i-muh, fa-TEE-muh)   Muslim female name that is very popular in North Africa. The name refers to one of Muhammed's daughters and means "weaned."

FATIMATA (fa-tee-MA-tuh)   A female name found in the Koran, the holy book of the Islamic religion, that is popular with the Diawara people of Mali.

FATUMA (fah-TOO-mah, FAH-too-mah, FAH-doo-mah)   Popular Swahili and Somali versions of the name **FATIMA** (see above).

FAYOLA (fah-YOH-lah)   Yoruba of Nigeria female name meaning "luck walks with honor."

FEMBAR (FEHM-bahr)   A female name from Liberia.

FIMI (FEE-mee)   A river in western Zaire that is 550 miles (880 kilometers) long and flows into Lake Mai-Ndombe. It is also known as the **FINI** (FEE-nee) and the **MFINI** (m-FEE-nee) River.

FOLA (FAW-lah, FOH-lah)   Yoruba of Nigeria female name meaning "honor."

FON (fawn)   A people numbering over one million living in Togo and southern Benin. The Fon ruled the Allada Kingdom in the sixteenth and seventeenth centuries A.D., and the Dahomey Kingdom in the seventeenth century A.D.

FOURAH (FOOR-ah)   Fourah Bay is near Freetown, the capital of Sierra Leone. It is site of Fourah Bay College, one of sub-Sahara Africa's oldest colleges.

FOWSIA (fow-SEE-uh)   Popular female name in Somalia.

FULA (FOO-lah)   A Mandingo word meaning "red." Used for the Fula ethnic group of West Africa, the name refers to the light brown color of their skin. The Fula are also known as the **FULBE** (FOOL-bay) and **FULFULDE**, or "red men."

Male

FANG (fang)   A Bantu language and people with a population over one million found in three West African countries: Cameroon, Equitorial Guinea, and Gabon. In Gabon, they constitute 25 percent of the population and are known for their fine traditional sculptures.

FARAJI (fah-RAH-jee)   Swahili male name meaning "consolation." Probably derived from **FARAJA** (fah-RAH-jah), the Kiswahili word with the same meaning.

FARIM (FAHR-im)   A town in northern Guinea-Bissau found on the Cacheu River.

FASILIDAS (fah-SEE-lee-duhs)   A former King of Ethiopia.

FDERIK (fee-DAIR-ik)   A town in Mauritania near the border with Western Sahara.

FELA (FAY-lah)   A West African male name meaning "warlike." Fela Anikulapo Kuti is a Nigerian musician and political dissident known as the King of Afro-Beat. He was born in 1941 in the town of Abeokuta by the name of Fela Ransome Kuti.

FEZ (fehz)   Also called **FES** (fehs), this residential city is the provincial capital of north central Morocco. Fez is the center of traditional Moroccan handicrafts, such as the Turkish hat which we know as a "fez." The souk, or market, in Fez is one of the world's largest. Fez was the capital of the Idrisid Kingdom, which was founded in 808 A.D. by Idris II, a descendent of the Islamic prophet Muhammed.

FODJOUR (FOH-djor)   An Akan of Ghana name for fourth-born boys.

FOGO (FOH-goh)   One of the southern Cape Verde islands with an active volcano. Islanders grow tobacco, oranges, and, reputedly, some of the world's finest coffee.

FRANCO (FRANG-koh)   The stage name of Francis L'Okanga La Ndju Pene Luambo Makiadi, a world-famous Zairois Congo jazz singer. His genre of music is called soukous, which means "having a good time." He became known as the Grand Sorcerer of the Guitar. Franco sang in both French and Lingala backed by his thirty-seven-piece T.P.O.K. Jazz Band. (The T.P. stands for the French phrase "tout puissant" meaning "all powerful.")

FRUMENTIUS (froo-MEHN-shi-uhs)   The Catholic patron saint of Ethiopia. Born in Tyre, an ancient city in modern-day Lebanon, Frumentius traveled to Ethiopia where he introduced Christianity to the Kingdom of Axum in the fourth century A.D. His feast day is October 27.

FYNN (feen)   This Ghanaian male name is an Europeanized version of the male name Offin, after the Offin River.

G

If stretching were wealth, the cat would be rich.
— Ghanaian proverb

Female

GABBRA (GA-bruh)   A nomadic, camel-herding people of the Chalbi Desert in northern Kenya. The Gabbra were formerly subjugated by Borana tribes who migrated from Ethiopia.

GABRI (GAH-bree)   A people of Chad whose language belongs in the Somrai language group.

GARBA TULLA (GAHR-bah TOO-lah)   A town in the Garissa District of northern Kenya that is a main center for the Gabbra people.

GARISSA (gahr-IS-sah)   A market town in the North East Province of Kenya near the Somali border on the Tana River.

GEMENA (gay-MAY-nah)   A town in northern Zaire.

GENEINA (jeh-NAY-nah)   A Sudanese town in Darfur Province near the border of Chad.

GEZIRA (juh-ZEER-uh)   a) Also spelled **JAZIRA** or **EL JEZIRA,** this geographical area between the Blue Nile and the White Nile south of Khartoum, Sudan, is home to large-scale irrigation projects, including the largest cotton growing and ginning project in Africa. Covering over one million acres, Gezira is irrigated by Nile waters. b) Gezira is a beach near Mogadishu, the capital of Somalia.

GIZA (GEE-zuh)   Also spelled **GIZEH,** a town adjacent to Cairo, Giza is home to the three Great Pyramids, including the Great Pyramid of Cheops and the Sphinx, which were built during the Fourth Egyptian Dynasty (2613–2494 B.C.). Also, Giza is a Teutonic female name meaning "gift."

GOGO (GOH-goh) A Tonga and Shona of Zambia of Zimbabwe word meaning "grandmother."

GUELMA (gehl-MAH, GWEL-mah) A manufacturing and crossroads town in northern Algeria. It was the site of an ancient Punic-Roman town called Calama.

GYAMFUA (jam-FOO-uh) Ashanti of Ghana female name.

GZIFA (gee-FAH) An Ewe of Ghana name meaning "one is at peace."

Male

GABON (ga-BOHN) The country of Gabon is crossed by the equator and shouldered by the Atlantic Ocean. It is mostly tropical forest-covered highlands. Gabon is 102,250 square miles (261,760 square kilometers) in size, making it somewhat smaller than Kentucky. Agriculture is the main economic activity, with cassava as the primary food crop. Some mining and forestry contribute to the economy. The country's name is derived from the original name used for the area by Portuguese explorers, Gabao, which means "sailor's cape."

GABORONE (gah-buh-ROHN, gah-buh-ROH-nee) Gaborone became the capital of Botswana in 1962. This city was named after a nineteenth-century chief of the area named Gaborone Matlapin.

GABRA Another spelling of the Ethiopian male name Gebre. Gabra Mika'el (1791–1855) was an Ethiopian monk. He is a Catholic saint whose feast day is September 1.

GARIAN (gah-ree-EHN) A town in northern Libya where troglodytes live in hillside caves or underground in man-made wells.

GARSEN (gahr-SEHN) A busy crossroads town in eastern Kenya on the Tana River populated mostly by Galla peoples.

GASTON (GAS-tuhn)   Gaston Berger was a Senegalese philosopher born in the city of Saint-Louis, where a university is named after him. Gaston is a French male name meaning "man of Gascony."

GEBEL MUSA (JEHB-uhl MOO-suh)   This mountain in Egypt is where Moses is believed to have received the Ten Commandments from God. There are three thousand steps cut into the side of this 7,497-foot-high (2,285 meters) mountain for persons making a pilgrimage to the chapel on the summit. The name is Arabic for "Mount Moses."

GEBRE (GUH-bruh)   Amharic and Tigrinya male name meaning "an offering." This name is usually used in combination with other names. For example, **GEBRE YESUS** (GUH-bruh YAY-soos) means "offered in servitude to Jesus" and **GEBRE MIKAEL** (GUH-bruh MEEK-ah-ayl) means "offered in servitude to the angel Michael."

GEDI (GEHD-ee)   Historical ruins on the Kenyan coast ten miles from the town of Malindi. Constructed of coral stone masonry, it was once a thriving provincial Swahili town which reached its height in the mid-1400s. It was abandoned in the early 1600s due to the southern movement of Galla nomads from Somalia. The town's name is derived from the Galla word and personal name Gede, which means "precious."

GELASIUS (guh-LAY-zee-oos, jeh-LAY-shi-us)   Although Gelasius I was born in Rome, his father, Valerius, was an African. Gelasius I became the Pope in 492 A.D. He is a Catholic saint whose feast day is November 21.

GETACHEW (gay-tah-CHOW)   Amharic male name meaning "their master."

GETEYE (gay-TEE-yay)   Amharic male name meaning "my master."

GHALI (GAH-lee)   A Kiswahili word meaning "expensive, scarce," and a Muslim male name meaning "precious."

GHANA (GAHN-uh, GA-nuh)   Meaning "war chief," this title was used for early kings of the area that is now the country of Ghana.

GHEDI (GEHD-ee)   A Somali male name meaning "traveler."

GIADO (gee-AH-doh)   A town in northern Libya.

GOGO (GOH-goh)   a) Nguni of South Africa male name meaning "like grandfather." b) A people of Tanzania who speak a Bantu language. c) A Kiswahili noun meaning "log."

GONDAR (GON-dahr)   Found beside Lake Tana in the north of Ethiopia, Gondar was the capital of the Amhara Empire from the 1600s through the 1800s. Several Ethiopian emperors built castles in the town, making it a tourist attraction.

GUEDADO (gwee-DAH-doh)   Fulani of Mali name for both males and females that means "wanted by nobody."

GYAMFI (jahm-FEE)   Ashanti of Ghana male name.

H

"...thou, O daughter of Hathor, are made to triumph, thy head shall never be taken away from thee and thou shalt be made to rise up in peace."

—Ancient text

Female

HABESHA (hah-BUHSH-ah)   The name of the Semitic peoples of the highlands of Ethiopia. The Habesha are descendants of inhabitants of the ancient kingdom of Axum. They spoke Ge'ez, an Ethio-Semitic language, and had a thriving international trading economy.

HABIBA (hah-BEE-bah)   Muslim female name popular in Somalia and North Africa meaning "beloved, sweetheart."

HADIYA (hah-DEE-yah, HAH-dee-yah)   Also spelled **HADIYAH**, Swahili female name meaning "gift," and Muslim female name meaning "guide to righteousness."

HALIMA (hah-LEE-mah)   Also spelled **HALIMAH**, this Swahili and Muslim female name means "gentle, humane, kind" and refers to the Prophet Muhammed's nurse. It is a popular name in Egypt and Somalia.

HARBEL (hahr-BEHL)   A town on the Farmington River near Monrovia, Liberia.

HASANA (hah-SAH-nah)   Hausa of West Africa name for the firstborn of twins when it is a female.

HASINA (hah-SEE-nah)   Swahili female name meaning "good."

49

HASSIBA (hah-SEE-buh)   Muslim female name used in North Africa. Hassiba Boulmerka won Algeria's first Olympic gold medal in 1992 for the 1500-meter run with a time of 3:55.30.

HATHOR (HATH-or)   An Egyptian name meaning "temple of Horus." Hathor is the Egyptian goddess of joy and love and the protector of women. She is also called the "Lady of Turquoise" and the "Lady of the Sycamore." Hathor is usually represented as a woman with cow's ears and horns on her head with a solar disk lodged in the horns. A large rock-hewn temple dedicated to Hathor, built under Ramses II some three thousand years ago, is found in Abu Simbel in southern Egypt.

HAWA (HAH-wah, HOW-uh)   Swahili female name meaning "longing."

HERA (HIER-uh)   According to Greek mythology, Hera is Zeus's sister and wife and she is the goddess of women, marriage, and sex. Hera means "lady."

HOLA (HOH-lah)   An Ewe of Ghana name meaning saviour."

HOMA (HOH-mah)   a) Homa Bay is a fishing village in Kenya on Lake Victoria. b) A very small ethnic group in Sudan that speak a Bantu language. c) A Kiswahili word meaning "fever."

HOVA (HOH-vah)   The name used for the middle class, or commoner class, of the Betsileo people of central Madagascar.

HUDA (HOO-dah)   Muslim female name that is popular in Egypt. It means "proper guidance."

Male

HABIB (hah-BEEB)   Popular in North Africa, this is a Swahili and Muslim male name meaning "beloved." Habib Ben Ali Bourguiba, the first President of Tunisia, was born in 1903 and was educated in Tunis and Paris.

HAGOS (HAH-gohs)   Tigrinya of Ethiopia male name meaning "joy, happiness."

HAJI (HAH-jee)   Swahili name for males born during the hajj, or the period when Muslims make pilgrimage to Mecca.

HAKI (HAH-kee)   A Kiswahili word meaning "justice."

HAKIM a) (HAH-keem)   Amharic and Tigrinya of Ethiopia male name meaning "doctor, medicine man." It is most commonly used by Muslim Ethiopians. b) (hah-KEEM or HA-kim)   A Muslim male name that is popular in the Sudan and means "wise."

HANIF (HAH-neef)   Swahili and Muslim male name meaning "believer."

HANISI (hah-NEE-see)   Swahili name for males born on Thursday.

HARCOURT (HAHR-kurt, HAHR-cohrt)   Port Harcourt is a principal city of Nigeria located on the Niger River delta on the southern edge of Iboland. It was founded in 1912 during World War I and was named after a minister in the English colonial government. Harcourt is a European male name that comes from the Teutonic and means "fortified residence."

HARI (HAH-ree)   A Kiswahili word meaning "heat." Also, Hari is a Hindu male name that refers to the Lord Vishnu.

HARPER (HAHR-puhr)   A coastal city in Liberia near the border with Cote D'Ivoire. Harper is an old English male name for "one who plays the harp."

HASSAN (HAH-sahn)   a) Hausa of West Africa male name for the firstborn of twins. b) Muslim male name popular in North Africa that means "handsome." Muhammed Abdilleh Hassan was a twentieth-century Somali leader who was a revered poet in his country. Europeans dubbed him the "Mad Mullah."

HASSANI (hah-SAHN-nee)   Swahili variation of the Muslim male name **HASSAN** which means "handsome."

HEIBAN (HAY-bahn)   A people living in the Nuba Hills in Sudan who
speak a dialect of Koalib-Tagoi.

HEKANEFER (hehk-AN-ehf-ur)   An Egyptian name meaning "the good prince." Ancient Egyptians gave this name to a Nubian chief who was the Prince of Miam, an Egyptian colonial outpost in northern Nubia (now northern Sudan).

HERI (HAY-ree)   This Kiswahili word means "happiness." The way to say good-bye in Kiswahili is "kwa heri," literally meaning "with happiness."

HIJI (HEE-jee)   A Kiswahili word meaning "to make a pilgrimage." Also, a West African male name.

HOGAN (HOH-gahn)   An Efik of Nigeria male name of uncertain origin, but it was probably introduced by Portuguese traders hundreds of years ago. Hogan "Kid" Bassey was born in 1932 in Calabar, Nigeria. Hogan won Nigeria's flyweight boxing title at age seventeen. In 1957 he won the world featherweight championship. Hogan made his home in Liverpool, England.

HONDO (HOHN-doh)   A Zezuru (sub-group of the Shona-speaking peoples) of Zimbabwe male name meaning "war."

HOSEA (hoh-ZAY-uh)   Hosea Kutako was chief of the Herero people of northeast Namibia. In 1946 he led his people in petitioning the United Nations to guarantee their political freedom from South Africa. Hosea is a male name of Hebrew origin meaning "salvation."

HUSANI (hoo-SAHN-ee)   Swahili variation of the Muslim male name **HUSAYN** which means "beautiful."

I

Ismitta, the embodiment of the southern wind is...a beautiful, slender negro-girl, intimately close to the divine images of the sources of the Nile in the Egyptian mind which goes back to ancient Egyptian cosmology. She is the "daughter of the Mountains of the Moon" whose laughter is lightning and whose tears are torrential rains.
—Unknown North African poet, from Ali A. Mazrui's
The Africans: A Triple Heritage

Female

IFEOMA (ee-feh-OH-mah) Ibo of Nigeria female name meaning "it's a good thing" and "beautiful."
IKEJA (ee-KAY-yuh) The capital city of Lagos State, Nigeria.
ILA (EE-lah) A people of southern Zambia and the name of their Bantu language. Also, in Kiswahili ila means "except."
ILESHA (i-LEE-shah, i-LEHSH-uh) A city in Oyo State, Nigeria. The city's main economic activity is brewing.
ILLELA (ee-LAY-lah) Town in Niger that was formerly the Tuareg capital of the Adar region in the seventeenth century.
ILORIN (i-LAWR-uhn, ee-luh-REEN) A market town and the capital of Kwara State in southwestern Nigeria. This mud-walled city is the main trading center for the Yoruba peoples and is known for its pottery. (Could be shortened to **LORIN**.)
IMAN (ee-MAHN) Somali and Muslim female name meaning "faith." Iman is a well-known high-fashion model and

actress from Somalia who was "discovered" while living in Nairobi, Kenya.

IMANA (ee-MAHN-ah) a) Meaning "almighty," this is the supreme god and god of creation for the Batutsi people of Rwanda and Burundi. b) A Hausa word meaning "protection."

IMANI (ee-MAHN-ee) The Kiswahili word for "faith."

IMARA (ee-MAHR-ah) A Kiswahili word meaning "solid, firm."

IMERINA (i-MAIR-i-nuh) A highland town inhabited mainly by Merina people, this is the regional capital of central Madagascar.

IMI (EE-mee) A town on the Shebelle River in central Ethiopia.

INDRI Numbering only a few hundred, the Indri people live in southern Sudan's Rega region. They speak a language of the Feroge language group.

IRAS (IGH-ruhs) A loyal African servant of Cleopatra. The name Iras was used in ancient Egypt for persons having the trait of woolly hair.

ISADORA (iz-uh-DOR-uh) Also spelled **ISIDORA**, **DORA**, and **IDORA**, this female Egyptian name refers to the goddess Isis and means "gift of Isis." (See ISIS below.)

ISALA (ee-SAH-lah) These people, also called **SISALA**, are found in northern Ghana and in Burkina Faso. They speak a dialect from the Gur language.

ISANDRA (i-SAHN-drah) City in central Madagascar.

ISHARA (ee-SHAH-rah) A Kiswahili word defined as "a signal, a sign."

ISIMILA (ee-see-MEE-lah) A prehistoric site near the town of Iringa in southern Tanzania.

ISIS (IGH-sis) Female Egyptian name meaning "seat, throne" referring to the mythological goddess Isis. Isis is the goddess of fertility and birth and is guardian of the Nile River. Legend tells that the Nile was created by the gushing tears of Isis when her brother and husband Osiris was killed. According to the *Book of the Dead*, texts from ancient Egypt, Isis is a black woman. She is depicted with cow horns on her head inside of which is a sun disk, like Hathor, or with a throne on her head. Isis was also worshipped by people of the ancient kingdom of Meroë (in present-day Sudan).

ISMAILIA (iz-may-uh-LEE-uh)   Also spelled **ISMAILIYA**. A city on the Suez Canal beside Lake Timsah south of Port Said in northeast Egypt. Ismailia was founded in 1863 during the construction of the Suez Canal. The city got its name from Ismail Pasha, a Turkish ruler of Egypt at the time.

ISMITTA (is-MI-tuh)   A mythical North African name for the southern wind, which means "Daughter of the Mountains of the Moon."

ISSA (EE-sah)   A Swahili name meaning "God is our salvation."

ISSA BERI (EE-sah BAIR-ee)   The Songhai name for the Niger River, which means "river of rivers."

ISHI (UH-shee)   The word for "yes" in the Amharic language of Ethiopia.

IVA (EEV-ah)   A Kiswahili word meaning "to ripen."

IVEREM (ee-VAIR-ehm)   Tiv of Nigeria female name meaning "blessing, favor."

IYANGURA (ee-yahn-GOOR-ah)   An unusual Nyanja of Zambia name meaning either "to arbitrate" or "to perform ceremonies for the birth of twins."

Male

IBRAHIM (EE-brah-heem)   Hausa of West Africa male name meaning "father is exalted." Also, Ibrahim is the Muslim variation of the Hebrew name Abraham, which means "father of a multitude." Ibrahim Babangida became president of Nigeria in 1985.

IDI (EE-dee)   Swahili and Muslim name for males born during the Muslim holiday of Idd, which marks the end of Ramadan, the ninth month of the Muslim year highlighted by daily fasting.

IDRIS (i-DREES)   a) Idris I was the King of Libya from independence in 1951 to the revolution of 1969. He led Libya's fight for independence from Italy. b) Idris Alooma was the King of Kanem-Bornu (part of present-day northern Nigeria) from 1571 to 1603. He was known for spreading Islam and building mosques throughout his kingdom. c) Idris Ibn Adb Allah founded the Idrisids Dynasty in northern Morocco in A.D. 788. He claimed to be a descendent of Muhammed through Muhammed's son-in-law, Caliph Ali. He was poisoned in A.D. 795 by Harun al Rashid.

IDRISSA (ee-DREES-ah)   A male name from Senegal and the Gambia meaning "immortal."

IKHET (ik-HEHT)   Ancient Egyptian word meaning "the glorious."

IMO (EE-moh)   One of the nineteen states of Nigeria. Imo is in southern Nigeria and has a population over six million. Its capital city is Owerri.

INIKO (ee-NEE-Koh)   Efik and Ibibio of Nigeria name for males and females born amidst civil war or other troubled times.

ISKINDER (uhs-KUHN-dur)   Amharic of Ethiopia version of the Greek name Alexander which means "defender or helper of mankind."

ISMAIL (is-mah-EEL)   The Muslim name for the biblical Moses. King Ismail ruled the Sennar Empire located on the Blue Nile River in Abyssinia (present-day Ethiopia) in the late eighteenth century.

ISSA (ee-SAH)   a) Swahili and Muslim male name meaning "the Messiah" and referring to Jesus as a prophet. b) The Issa people live in southern Djibouti, are ethnically related to the Somalis, and speak a dialect of Somali. c) Abdullahi Issa was a founder of Somalia's primary independence party. He served as the first Prime Minister of Somalia's parliament in 1959, and held many high government positions until 1969 when he was jailed.

IYASU (ee-YAH-soo)   Amharic and Tigrinya of Ethiopia male name. Known as Iyasu the Great, this Christian emperor ruled Abyssinia (modern Ethiopia) from 1682 until he was murdered in 1706. Iyasu II ruled from 1730–1755.

IZI BONGO (I-zee BOHN-goh) Folk songs praising the history and achievements of the Zulu peoples of South Africa.

J

When the missionaries came the Africans had the land and the Christians had the Bible. They taught us to pray with our eyes closed. When we opened them they had the land and we had the Bible.
—Jomo Kenyatta, first President of Kenya

Female

JADIDA (juh-DEE-duh) Also called **AL-JADIDA**, this seaport and resort town on the west coast of Morocco was established in 1502.

JADINI (jah-DEE-nee) The Jadini Forest is found south of Mombasa, Kenya. It is home to baboons, colobus monkeys, and an abundance of bird life.

JAGA (JAH-gah) Founded in the sixteenth century, this kingdom was located in modern Zaire.

JAHA (JAH-hah) Swahili female name meaning "dignity" and Kiswahili word meaning "good fortune."

JAINEBA (jay-NEE-bah) A female name popular with the Wolof people of Senegal.

JALIA (jah-LEE-ah) Kiswahili word meaning "to grant."

JAMA (JAH-mah) A female name popular with the Wolof people of Senegal.

JAMILA (jah-MEE-lah) Popular in Somali, Swahili, and Arabic cultures, this female name means "beautiful, elegant."

JANA (JAH-nah) Kiswahili word for "yesterday." Pronounced YAH-nah, it is a female Eastern European name meaning "God's gracious gift."

JANI (JAH-nee)   Kiswahili word for "a leaf."

JAPERA (juh-PAIR-uh)   Shona of Zimbabwe female name meaning "offer thanks."

JAZA (JAH-zah)   Kiswahili word meaning "to fill."

JABAL KATRINAH (JAB-uhl kuh-TREE-nuh)   Also **GEBEL KATHERINA** (JEHB-uhl kath-uh-REE-nuh). A mountain in northeastern Egypt that is 8,652 feet (2,637 meters) high. According to legend, the body of Saint Katherine of Alexandria was brought by angels to this mountaintop. The name is Arabic for "Mount Catherine."

JIFUNZA (jee-FOON-zah)   A Kiswahili word and Swahili name meaning "teach oneself."

JINA (JEE-nah)   Kiswahili word for "a name." Also, a Buddhist title meaning "conqueror."

JINI (JEE-nee)   Kiswahili word meaning "a genie."

JINJA (JIN-juh)   The second largest city in Uganda located in the southeast region of the country on Lake Victoria. Jinja is near Owens Falls and is a major military and industrial center.

JIONA (jee-OH-nah)   A Kiswahili word meaning "to be vain."

JIONI (jee-OH-nee)   A Kiswahili word for "evening."

JOHARI (joh-HAHR-ee)   A Kiswahili word for "jewel."

JOLA (JOH-lah)   A peoples of Senegal and the Gambia.

JOLIBA (JAHL-uh-buh)   The local name for the 2,600-mile (4,160 kilometers) Niger River. It means "the great stream." (Could be shortened to **JOLI**.)

JUBA (joo-BAH)   Ashanti of Ghana name for females born on Monday.

JWAHIR (WAH-heer, jeh-WAH-hair)   Somali female name meaning "golden woman."

Male

JAFARI (jah-FAHR-ee)   Swahili male name meaning "creek." It is a variation of the Muslim name **JAFAR**.

JAHI (JAH-hee)   Swahili male name meaning "dignity."

JAJA (JAH-jah)   Ibo of Nigeria male name meaning "God's gift" or "honored."

JAKOBI (jah-KOH-bee)   A Mandinka of West Africa word meaning "star."

JAMAL (jeh-MEHL)   This Muslim male name is popular in the Sudan and means "beautiful, graceful."

JAWARA (juh-WAHR-ah)   Male name from Senegal and the Gambia meaning "peace loving."

JEBEL MUSA (JEHB-uhl MOO-suh)   This mountain in northern Morocco is located opposite the Rock of Gibraltar across the Strait of Gibraltar. Together these two mountains are known as "The Pillars of Hercules."

JEFREN (JEHF-rehn)   A picturesque Berber town in Libya graced by a hilltop castle.

JELA (JAY-lah)   This Swahili male name means "father was suffering during birth" and probably stems from the Swahili word "jela," which is a corruption of the English word "jail," meaning "prison."

JIMA (JEE-muh)   An Ethiopian male name. Also, spelled **JIMMA** or **GIMMA**, it is a town in southwest Ethiopia where coffee grows wild in the rain forests. The capital of Kefa Province, it is the center of Ethiopia's coffee-growing area and the main center for the Muslim Oromo people.

JIMBO (JEEM-boh)   Kiswahili word for "country, province."

JIMIYU (JEE-mee-yoo)   Luhya of Kenya name used for males born during the dry season. (Could be shortened to **JIMI**.)

JIRANI (jee-RAH-nee)   A Kiswahili word meaning "neighbor." (Could be shortened to **RANI**.)

JIRI (JEER-ee)   Zezuru people of Zimbabwe male name meaning "forest of wild fruits." Jiri is also the Czechoslovakian version of the male name George.

JOJO (JOH-joh)   A Europeanized version of the Fante and Ashanti of Ghana traditional names **KOJO** and **KWADJO** which are used for males born on Monday.

JOMO (JOH-moh)   A Gikuyu of Kenya male name meaning "farmer." Jomo Kenyatta (1893–1978) was author of the classic anthropological book, *Facing Mount Kenya,* which was published in 1938. In 1963 he became the first President of Kenya. As President, Kenyatta earned the title "Mzee," a Kiswahili name of respect for the elderly.

JOS (jawz; rhymes with "boss")   Situated on the high, fertile Jos plateau, Jos is the capital of Benue-Plateau State in north central Nigeria.

JOZI (JOH-zee)   Kiswahili word meaning "a pair."

JUBA (JOO-buh)   a) Juba was King of Numidia, an ancient state of North Africa, from 62–46 B.C. b) The regional capital of southern Sudan, located on the White Nile River. c) The southern region of Somalia, as well as the 1,000-mile (1,609 kilometers) river that flows through it, starting in Ethiopia and flowing into the Indian Ocean.

JUGURTHA (joo-GUR-thuh)   King of the ancient North African state of Numidia in the second century B.C., King Jugurtha attacked Rome in an unsuccessful bid to fight off Roman annexation of his kingdom.

JULIUS (JOOL-ee-uhs, JOOL-yuhs)   This Greek male name meaning "soft-haired and downy-bearded," which symbolizes youth, is popular in East Africa. a) Julius Kambarage Nyerere was the first president of independent Tanzania and a former chairman of the Organization of African Unity (OAU). He became revered in Tanzania and worldwide for his egalitarian leadership principles. In Tanzania he is called "Mwalimu (mwah-LEE-moo)," the Kiswahili word meaning "teacher," a name of respect. Nyerere is also a political philosopher and author. He translated Shakespeare's *Julius Caesar* and *The Merchant of Venice* into Kiswahili. b) Julius Korir of Kenya won the gold medal in the 1984 Olympics for the 3,000-meter steeplechase with a time of 8:11.8.

JUMA (JOO-mah)   Swahili name for males born on Friday. The Muslim spelling of the same name is **JUMAH**. Also, in Kiswahili the word "juma" means "a week."

K

A plaque at the summit of Mount Kilimanjaro in Tanzania reads:

We the people of Tanzania would like to light a candle and put it on top of Mount Kilimanjaro which would shine beyond our borders, giving hope where there is despair, love where there is hate, and dignity where before there was only humiliation.

Female

KADIJA (kah-DEE-jah)   Also spelled **KHADIJA**, this Swahili female name refers to the Prophet Muhammed's first wife. It means "born prematurely." The Muslim and Somali pronunciation of the name is kah-dee-YAH.

KAEDI (kah-AYD-ee)   A town on the Senegal River in southern Mauritania.

KAHINA (KAH-hee-nah)   Berber leader and prophetess. Princess Kahina organized a confederacy of Berber tribes which descended from the Atlas Mountains in Algeria to fight off Arab invaders who had gained control of much of northern Africa. Despite her fierce resistance, she was defeated and killed in the final battle at Tabarka, Tunisia in A.D. 703.

KAHIRAH (kah-HEER-ah)   Also called **AL-QAHIRAH**, this Arabic name for the city of Cairo, Egypt, means "the victorious."

KALI (KAH-lee)   A Kiswahili word meaning "fierce, sharp." Also, a female name derived from Sanskrit meaning "energy" and referring to a Hindu goddess named SAKTI. Sakti, the goddess of creation and destruction, is depicted as being black-skinned.

KALINA (kuh-LEE-nuh) A residential area of Kinshasa, Zaire's capital city.

KAMA (KAH-mah) A Kiswahili word meaning "if, whether, like." Also, an Indian female name meaning "love" and referring to the Hindu god of love who is depicted as being black-skinned.

KAMARIA (kah-mah-REE-ah) Swahili and Somali female name meaning "like the moon." It is related to the Muslim name **KAMRA**, which means "moon."

KAMBIRI (kahm-BEER-ee) Ibo of Nigeria female name meaning "allow me to join this family."

KAMINA (kuh-MEEN-uh) A city near Lubumbashi in Shaba Province, Zaire. Also, the name of a town in southern Togo.

KANIKA (kah-NEE-kah) A Kenyan female name meaning "black material," probably derived from the Kiswahili word **KANIKI** (kah-NEE-kee), which means "dark cotton cloth."

KANISA (kah-NEE-sah) Kiswahili word for "church."

KANYA (KAHN-yuh) The main city of the Bangwaketsi people of Botswana.

KARA (KAHR-uh) a) Ethnic groups named Kara are found in Uganda, Rwanda, Tanzania, and Equatoria Province, Sudan. b) The Kara River is in northern Togo. c) A version of the female name Cara, which is of Latin origin and means "dear."

KARATALA (kahr-uh-TAHL-uh) An active volcano on Great Comoro Island located in the Comoros off the southeast coast of Africa.

KARE (KAHR-ay) Bantu-speaking people who live in eastern Zaire and the Central African Republic.

KARI (KAHR-ee) A people found in Cameroon and Chad. Also, a short form of Caroline, which comes from Latin and means "womanly."

KARIBA (kuh-REE-buh) A lake in Zambia and Zimbabwe formed by the damming of the Zambezi River in 1958. The lake got its name from the Shona word **KARIWA,** which means "little trap" because of the way the river narrows when it reaches the Kariba Gorge. Lake Kariba is one of the world's largest man-made lakes.

KARIN (KAHR-in)   A town in northern Somalia on the Gulf of Aden. Also, a short form of the female name Katherine, which comes from Greek and means "pure."

KARMA (KAHR-mah)   A small market town on the Niger River, not far from Niamey, the capital of Niger. Also, Karma (KAHR-muh) is a Hindu and Buddhist word signifying "destiny," "fate," or "aura."

KARRI-KARRI (KAHR-ee KAHR-ee)   This local name for the Kalahari Desert of southern Africa means "suffering, torture, torment."

KASENA (kah-SEE-nah)   A people from northern Ghana.

KASSALA (KAS-uh-luh)   The capital of Kassala Province, this city in northeastern Sudan is beside the Ethiopian border. The town, built on very fertile land, was founded around 1840 as an Egyptian fort.

KASSERINE (kas-uh-REEN)   Also **AL-QASRAYN** (al-kahs-REEN). a) This Tunisian town is the site of a World War II battle in which the United States forces were victorious. It is also the site of ancient Roman ruins, which have not yet been extensively excavated. b) A town in Morocco.

KATSINA (KAHT-si-nuh)   Town in northern Nigeria near the Niger border. It is the former capital of the Kingdom of Katsina, an early Hausa state.

KATURA (kah-TOOR-ah)   A female and male name from Zimbabwe that means "take a burden off my mind."

KAYA (KAH-yah)   a) Ghanaian female name meaning "stay and don't go back." It comes from the Ga word meaning "don't go." Traditionally this name would be used in a family where some children have already died. b) Karimojong of northeast Uganda word for "cousin." c) A town in Burkina Faso. d) The name used by the Nyika people of coastal Kenya and Tanzania for fortified hilltop villages.

KAYA TIWI (KAH-yah TEE-wee)   This site, located to the north of Diani Beach on the Indian Ocean coast of Kenya, is a place of sanctuary for local residents.

KAYLA (KIGH-luh)   An Ethiopian ethnic group and the Cushitic language that they speak. These people are also called the **KAILINYA** (kigh-LEEN-yuh). Also, Kayla is used in the United States as a form of Kay or Katherine, which means "pure."

KEBBI (KEH-bee)   A town in northern Nigeria whose name originated from the former Kingdom of Kebbi which controlled the area in the sixteenth to nineteenth centuries. Kebbi is also a river in Nigeria.

KEBRA NEGAST (KUH-bruh NEH-guhst)   The title of this thirteenth-century book means "the Glory of Kings." The Kebra Negast records the history of Ethiopia's monarchs and makes the claim that the original Ark of the Covenant, the chest containing the stone tablets engraved with the Ten Commandments, is in Ethiopia. The book is written in Ge'ez, an ancient language of Ethiopia.

KELA (KAY-lah)   A people of the Kasai Province of Zaire who speak a Bantu language.

KENGI (kehn-GEE)   A Loma people of West Africa female name. Kengi is the subject of a Loma folktale called "Whose Child?"

KENITRA (kuh-NEE-truh)   This port city is in northwest Morocco near the Atlantic Ocean. Formerly called Port Lyautey, it was a landing site of U.S. troops during World War II.

KENYA (KEHN-yuh)   a) East African name meaning "artist." (Although it is a male name in East Africa, it has been used in the United States already as a female name.) b) One of Africa's best-known countries because of animal-safari tourism. Kenya's land area is 224,961 square miles (582,645 square kilometers). There are over forty different ethnic groups living in Kenya, most of whom engage in agriculture. Tourism and coffee exports are Kenya's major source of foreign income. c) Snow-capped Mount Kenya, located on the equator, is 17,058 feet (5,195 meters) high. The Kikuyu call this mountain **KERE-NYAGA**, which means "mountain of mystery." They believe the mountain is home to the Supreme God, Ngai.

KERA a) A people from Cameroon. b) (KAY-rah) A Kiswahili word meaning "to worry." c) MFK Kera is a female singer from Senegal.

KERAN Keran is the name of a national park in northern Togo as well as the name of a river in the park. **KERANI** (keh-RAH-nee) means "sacred bells" and is a popular name in India.

KEREN (KAR-uhn) This town, also called **CHEREN** (KAR-ayn), is found in Eritrea (a contested northern province of Ethiopia). Also, Keren is a Hebrew female name meaning "horn."

KESI (KAY-see) This Swahili female name means "born when the father had difficulties." The word "kesi" in Kiswahili means "lawsuit" and probably is a derivation of the English word "case."

KESS (kehs) A priest of the Ethiopian Orthodox Coptic Church. (This word is properly pronounced with a clicking sound on the K.)

KESSIE (keh-SEE-eh) Fante and Ashanti of Ghana female name meaning "born fat."

KHALIFA (kah-LEE-fah) Muslim female name that is popular in Somalia and means "holy girl."

KHATITI (kah-TEE-tee) Luhya of Kenya name for females and males meaning "tiny, little."

KIBIBI (kee-BEE-bee) Swahili name means "little lady." (In Kiswahili "ki" is used as a diminutive prefix and "bibi" is the word for lady; thus "little lady.") When pronounced chee-BEE-bee, it is a Runyankore of Uganda name that means "beautiful fat girl."

KIFLE (KEHF-lay) Ethiopian female name meaning "my class."

KILIMA NDSCHARO (kee-LEE-mah ndSHAHR-oh) One of the local names for the highest mountain in Africa that was Anglicized to become Mount Kilimanjaro. The name is believed to come from the Kiswahili, meaning "hill of the demon of cold," "mountain of the caravans," or "great mountain." Others believe it is an ancestral name of the Chagga people who live near the foot of the mountain.

KIM (keem) A people from Chad who speak a language from the Somrai language group. Also, Kim is a short form of the English name Kimberly which means "ruler of the royal fortress."

KIMBAVETA (kim-bah-VEHT-uh) This Christian martyr from the Kingdom of the Congo was also known as **DONNA BEATRICE**. Her attempts to reform, or Africanize, the Christian church resulted in her being burned at the stake with her baby boy in 1706.

KINSHASA (kin-SHAHS-uh) Formerly called Leopoldville, Kinshasa is the capital city of Zaire. It is located on the east bank of the Zaire River and is a major industrial area. (Could be shortened to **SHASA**.)

KISSA (kis-AH) Baganda of Uganda name for female and male children born after twins.

KOKO (KOH-koh, koh-KOH) a) An Adangbe of Ghana name for second-born females. b) Koko Ateba is a Cameroonean singer whose first album was recorded in 1987 in Paris. c) A city in northwestern Nigeria. d) A Japanese female name meaning "stork."

KORA (KOHR-ah) a) Also called **KORANA**, these are a Hottentot-speaking people found in South Africa's Griqualand West. b) Kora National Reserve is located in the Tana River area in central Kenya. c) A Kora is a lute (a stringed musical instrument) with thirty-six strings played by West African traditional historians and poets who are called griots. d) A Greek female name meaning "maiden."

KWACHA (KWAHCH-ah) A unit of currency in Zambia whose name means "dawn."

KWANZA (KWAHN-zah) a) A six-hundred-mile-long (960-kilometer) river in Angola that flows into the Atlantic Ocean. b) A unit of currency in Angola. c) A Kiswahili word for "first" which was adopted by Maulana Ron Karenga, an

67

African-American university professor, as the name for a celebration of African heritage and culture. Kwanza runs from December 26 to January 1.

Male

KAARIA (kah-REE-uh)   A Kenyan male name meaning "one who speaks softly but with wisdom."

KABAKA (kuh-BAHK-uh)   The name used for kings of the Buganda people of Uganda.

KABWE (KAHB-way)   A town in central Zambia formerly known as Broken Hill. Also, a Zairean surname.

KAFA (KAF-uh, KAHF-uh, kuh-FAH)   Also known as **KAFFA, GOMARA,** and **KEFA** (KEEF-uh), this southwestern province of Ethiopia was acquired in 1897 from Muslim rulers. Kafa's main economic activity is coffee growing. The word "coffee" is believed to have originated from the name of this province.

KAIROUAN (kur-WAHN)   Also spelled **KAIRWAN** (kee-ur-WAHN) and **QAIRWAN** (keer-WAHN), this Muslim holy city is found in northeastern Tunisia.

KALEB (KAH-lehb)   An Amharic and Tigrinya of Ethiopia male name referring to the biblical Cain. Kaleb was Emperor of the Christian Kingdom of Axum (now northern Ethiopia) from A.D. 514–542.

KALENJIN (KAL-ehn-jin)   A highland people of Nilo-Hamitic origin who live in Kenya. The Kalenjin constitute about 11 percent of the country's population. (This name could be shortened to **KAL** or **KALEN.**)

KALIF (kah-LIF)   A Muslim male name that is popular in Somalia and means "holy boy."

KALUME (kah-LOO-may)   A name for male children of the Giriami people of coastal Kenya.

KAMALI (kah-MAHL-ee)   Shona people of Zimbabwe name that refers to a spirit who protects babies from death.

KAMALU (kah-MAH-loo)   An Ibo of Nigeria male name referring to the God of Lightning.

68

KAMAU (kah-MAH-oo, kah-MOW)   Kikuyu of Kenya male name meaning "quiet warrior."

KAMI (KAH-mee)   A people of eastern Tanzania who speak a Bantu language. Also, an Indian name meaning "desire," and referring to the Hindu god of love, who is depicted as black-skinned.

KAMILI (kah-MEE-lee)   Kiswahili word meaning "perfect, complete, flawless." It is related to the Muslim male names **KAMIL** (kah-MEEL) and **KAMAL** (kah-MAHL), which also mean "perfect."

KANO (KAH-noh)   This city in northern Nigeria was founded around A.D. 1,000 as the capital of a Hausa kingdom. The old quarters of this city are mud-walled. Kano was, and remains, an important trading center mostly populated by Hausa people.

KANTIGI (kahn-TEE-gee)   In the Mande language spoken in parts of Mali, "kantigi" means "a faithful person who keeps his word."

KAREEM (kah-REEM)   Popular in the Sudan, this Muslim male name means "generous."

KARNAK (KAHR-nak)   An ancient Egyptian temple which has pillars carved with hieroglyphics that recount the days of the pharaohs. The Temple of Karnak is over 2,000 years old and is located in the village of Karnak near Luxor, Egypt.

KASHKA (KAHSH-kah)   Nigerian male name meaning "friendly."

KASHTA (KAHSH-tuh)   This Nubian (meaning African) king ruled Egypt from around 760 to 747 B.C. Kashta was first in the line of Nubian kings constituting Egypt's XXV dynasty, which ruled for nearly one hundred years.

KASSA (KAH-sah)   Amharic male name meaning "compensation or reparation"; for instance, it could refer to a replacement for someone who has died.

KATO (KAH-toh)   Runyankore of Uganda name for a second-born twin who is male.

KAYA MAGHAN (kah-yah mah-GAHN)   A title used for early kings of what is now Ghana. It means "king of the gold."

KAYES (kayz)   A town in southwest Mali on the Senegal River.

KAYIN (kah-YEEN, kay-YIN)   Yoruba of Nigeria male name meaning "long-awaited child."

KAZEMBE (kah-ZAYM-bay)   The title used in the eighteenth century for rulers of a kingdom located on the Luapula River in modern-day northern Zambia.

KEITA (KAY-EE-tah, KAY-tah)   a) West African male name meaning "worshiper." b) A Guinean and Malian surname that indicates the family comes from the Malinke, or Mandingo, ethnic group. There are numerous prominent figures with the surname Keita: Sundiata Keita was the leader of the ancient Malian Empire before Mansa Musa; Fodeba Keita was founder of the Guinea National Ballet and was a politician and author; Modiba Keita was the president of Mali from 1960–1968 and was recipient of the Lenin Peace Prize in 1962; Salif Keita, nicknamed "Domingo," was a Malian football (soccer) player who received the African Footballer of the Year Award in 1970; another Salif Keita is a world-famous Malian musician. c) A town in Niger.

KELILE (kuh-LI-lay)   Amharic of Ethiopia male name meaning "my protector, my gate."

KEMANT (KUH-mahnt)   A people living in Gondar region of Northern Ethiopia who speak a Cushitic language.

KENAN (KAY-nahn)   Male name from Malawi.

KENYATTA (kehn-YAH-tuh)   East African male name meaning "musician." Jomo Kenyatta was the first president of Kenya.

KERICHO (kair-REE-choh)   A town in western Kenya known for its many tea plantations.

KEYO (KAY-oh)   Also called the **ELGEYO**, these people live in Kenya and speak a dialect of Kalenjin, a Nilo-Hamitic language.

KHALDUN (KEHL-doon, kahl-DOON)   A Muslim male name that is popular in North Africa and means "eternal."

KHAMISI (kah-MEE-see)   Swahili name for males born on Thursday.

KIFLE (KIF-lay)   An Amharic and Tigrinya male name that means "my share, my due."

KIJANA (kee-JAHN-ah)   A Kiswahili word meaning "youth, kid" which is used affectionately for young people.

KIMANE (kee-MAHN-ay)   Kikuyu of Kenya male name meaning "large bean."

KIMATHI (kee-MAH-thee)   A Kikuyu of Kenya male name meaning "earnest provider." It is also a common Kikuyu surname.

KIMBANGU (kim-BAHN-goo)   Simon Kimbangu of the Congo (now Zaire) was a prophet who attempted to put an African twist on Christianity in the 1920s. Although he spent thirty years in a Belgian colonial jail, where he also died, Kimbanguism and its Church of Jesus Christ on Earth is alive and well in central Africa. There are an estimated four million adherents, mostly in Zaire. (Could be shortened to **KIM**, itself an Old English male name meaning "chief.")

KIPCHOGE (kip-CHOH-gay)   Kipchoge "**Kip**" Keino was a Kenyan athlete who won the Olympic gold medal in 1968 for the 1,500-meter run with a time of 3:34.9 and in 1972 for the 3,000-meter steeplechase with a time of 8:23.6. Keino is from the Kalenjin ethnic group.

KIPSIGIS   A people of Kenya living east of Lake Victoria. They are traditionally farmers and cattle herders and speak a Nilo-Hamitic language. (Could be shortened to **KIP**.)

KIRDI   A mountain-dwelling people of northern Cameroon. Intolerant Muslim neighbors bestowed them with the name Kirdi, which means "infidels." The Kirdi, who live in the Mandara Mountains, practice subsistence agriculture on terraced slopes, with major crops being millet, peanuts, and beans.

KITABA (kee-TAH-bah)   According to the Basogo people of Uganda, Kitaba is a god who creates earthquakes by walking quickly. (Could be shortened to **KIT**.)

KITO (KEE-toh)   A Swahili male name meaning "precious" and a Kiswahili word for "jewel."

KIVU (KEE-voo)   Lake Kivu is found in northeast Zaire by the Rwandan border.

KOBI (KOH-bee)   A people living in the Ruwenzori Mountains in Uganda. They speak a Bantu language.

KOFI (koh-FEE)   One of the most common male names in Ghana, it is an Akan name used for children born on Friday. Pronounced KOH-fee, it is a Kiswahili word referring to the open hand. For instance, "piga makofi" translates as "to clap" or literally as "to hit the open hands."

KOJO (koh-JOH)   Ashanti of Ghana name for males born on Monday.

KOOFREY (KOH-free)   An Ibibio and Efik of Nigeria male name meaning "don't forget me."

KORFA (KOHR-fuh)   A Somali male name.

KOROLI (kuh-ROH-lee)   The Koroli Desert is found in northern Kenya south of Lake Turkana.

KRESH   A people who live in Equatoria Province, southern Sudan, and speak Bongo-Bagirmi.

KUKU (KOO-koo)   A people living on the Kajo Keji Plateau in southern Sudan and in Uganda. The Kuku speak a Nilo-Hamitic language. Also, the word "kuku" means "chicken" in Kiswahili and is used as a child's pet name.

KUMI (KOO-mee)   Akan of Ghana male name meaning "forceful." It is also the Kiswahili word for the number ten.

KURTEY   Relatives of the Songhai people who speak the Songhai language. The Kurtey are found in western Nigeria and Mali.

KWABENA (kwah-BEE-nah)   Akan of Ghana name for males born on Tuesday.

KWAKU (KWAH-koo)   Akan of Ghana name for males born on Wednesday and the name of the three former Ashanti kings.

KWAME (KWAH-meh, KWAH-mee)   This popular Akan of Ghana name is used for males born on Saturday. Kwame Nkrumah (1909–1972) became the first president of independent Ghana in 1960. Nkrumah was one of the leaders of Pan-Africanism. His book *Consciencism* speaks of the three influences that mold the African personality: traditional cultures, Islam, and European cultures. He was overthrown from the presidency in 1966 and went into exile in Guinea, where he died in 1972. Nkrumah is also author of *The Autobiography of Kwame Nkrumah* and *I Speak Freedom*.

KWAMI (KWAH-mee)   The Ewe of West Africa male name with the same meaning as Kwame (see above).

KWEKWE (KWAY-kway)   A town in central Zimbabwe.

KWESI (KWAY-see)   Akan of Ghana name for males born on Sunday.

L

The question in the air
on the shore
on the tongue of everyone
      -Luanda, where are you?

Silence in the streets
Silence in the tongues
Silence in the eyes
-Hey
sister Rose the fishwife
can you tell?

-Brother
I can't tell
have to sell
rush around the city
if you want to eat!

"Lu-u-nch, choose your lu-u-u-nch
sprats or mackerel
fine fish, fine fi-i-i-sh"
      —Excerpt from "Song for Luanda" by Angolan poet
                                    Luandino Vieira

Female

LAFIA (luh-FEE-uh)   A town in Benue-Plateau State in central Nigeria.
LALA (LAH-lah)   a) A Kiswahili word meaning "to sleep." b) A people of Zambia. c) A Slovakian (eastern Europe) name meaning "tulip."

LALI (LAH-lee)   A people from the Congo who speak a Bantu language.

LALIBELA (lah-lee-BEH-lah)   The capital of Ethiopia in the twelfth century A.D. This town is famous for eleven churches and chapels built underground from the solid stone of the Lasta Mountains by early Christians under the charge of King Gebra Maskal Lalibela of the Zagwe dynasty. King Lalibela is regarded as a saint in Ethiopia. Today Lalibela is primarily inhabited by Coptic priests and is sometimes referred to as Ethiopia's Jerusalem.

LAMIA (LAH-mee-uh)   According to Greek mythology, Zeus was in love with a beautiful vampire named Lamia. Lamia was a queen of African origin whose parents were Belus and Libya. Her Greek name means "gluttonous, lecherous, one who devours." Also, Lamia is a European name which is the feminine form of Lambert and means "brightness of the country."

LANDANA (lahn-DAHN-uh)   A city in Cabinda, a small, noncontiguous enclave of Angola. (Could be shortened to **LANA**, itself a version of the Greek female name Helen which means "light.")

LATEEFAH (lah-TEE-fah)   Popular in North Africa, this female Muslim name means "pleasant, gentle."

LAWRA (LAW-ruh)   A town in northern Ghana on the border with Burkina Faso.

LAYLA (LAH-ee-lah)   Also spelled **LAILA, LEYLA,** and **LEILA** (LIGH-lah).   A Swahili and Muslim female name meaning "born at night." Spelled **LEILAH,** it is a Persian name for those with dark hair.

LEA (LAY-ah)   A Kiswahili word defined as "to raise a child." Also, Lea is a Hebrew name meaning "weary" and an Assyrian name meaning "mistress" or "ruler."

LEALUI (LEE-uh-LOO-ee)   A town on the Zambezi River in Zambia.

LEBI (LAY-bee)   A people of Shaba Province, Zaire.

LELESHWA (leh-LAY-shwah)   A Kenyan name for wild sage plants.

LENANA (lay-NAH-nah)   One of the peaks of Mount Kenya, named after the son of a Masai chief. Lenana is the easiest peak to reach by amateur mountain climbers.

LENSHINA (layn-SHEEN-ah)   Alice Lenshina was a prophet from northern Rhodesia (now Zambia) who founded the reformed Christian Lumpa Church in 1953. At the age of twenty-nine, Lenshina was believed to have died and then been resurrected.

LETA (LAYT-ah)   Kiswahili word and Swahili name meaning "bring." Also, a European female name derived from Latin and meaning "gladness."

LEYA (LAY-yah)   A people from Zambia who speak a Bantu language. Pronounced LEH-yah, a Spanish female name meaning "law abiding."

LEZA (LAYZ-uh)   This name from central Africa means "one who besets" and refers to the mythological god of creation and of the sky.

LIA (LEE-ah)   Kiswahili word meaning "to cry." Also, a Hebrew and Italian female name meaning "dependence."

LINDA (LEEN-dah)   a) Xhosa of South Africa female name meaning "wait." b) A Kiswahili word meaning "to guard." c) A Spanish female name meaning "pretty, handsome." d) Teutonic female name meaning "lovely or gentle maid."

LINDI (LIN-dee)   a) A coastal town and region in southeastern Tanzania. b) A river in northeastern Zaire that is 375-miles (603 kilometers) long and flows into the Zaire River. c) A modern version of the female name Linda.

LINDIWE (lin-DEE-way)   Xhosa of South Africa female name meaning "have waited."

LISA   For the Fon people of Togo and southern Benin, Lisa is the sun god and god of creation whose form is a chameleon. Also, Lisa is a short form of the Hebrew name Elizabeth, which means "God's oath."

LISALA (lee-SAH-lah)   A town on the Congo River in northern Zaire.

LISHAN (LEE-shahn)   An Amharic female name meaning "award, medal." It has the same meaning as the Amharic name NISHAN.

LISSAWAN   A sedentary group of the Tuareg people who originated in the Air Mountains of Niger and went on to conquer the Adar region of Niger, making the town of Illela their capital in the seventeenth century. (Could be shortened to **LISSA**.)

LOI   A people of Zaire that speak a Bantu language.

LOIYAN (loy-YAHN)   A Masai of Kenya female name.

LOLA (LOH-lah)   A town in southern Guinea near the border with Cote D'Ivoire. Also, Lola is a Hawaiian version of the name Laura, meaning "crowned with laurels," and a short form of the Spanish name Carlota, which means "full-grown, strong."

LOMA (LOH-mah)   A people from Liberia and Guinea who speak a Mande language. Also, Loma is a short form of the Hebrew female name Salome that means "peaceful."

LOMELA (loh-MAY-luh)   A river in central Zaire. It flows 290 miles (464 kilometers) until it joins the Tshuapa River near Boende town.

LORIAN (LOHR-ee-uhn, LOR-ee-uhn)   A swamp in eastern Kenya into which the Ewaso Ng' iro River flows.

LORMA (LOR-muh)   A language spoken in Liberia.

LOTUS (LOH-tuhs)   Egyptian female name meaning "lily of the Nile."

LUANDA (loo-AHN-duh)   Also spelled **LOANDA** (loh-AHN-duh), Angola's capital city, founded in 1576, is the oldest city on Africa's west coast. Luanda is the country's main industrial area and has a deep-water port on the Atlantic Ocean. It is dubbed the "City of Bougainvilleas." The city's name is of local origin and possibly means "place of fishing nets" or "tribute," referring to the days when people collected shells as tribute, or taxes, for the king of the Kongo.

LUANSHYA (loo-AHN-shah)   A city in north-central Zambia near Lusaka, the capital. (Could be shortened to **LUAN**.)

LULU (LOO-loo)   A Swahili and Muslim female name meaning "pearl" or "precious." Also, Lulu is an English name meaning "a soothing influence."

LULUA (luh-LOO-uh)   A river running along the border of

Angola and Zaire. The river flows north for 550 miles (880 kilometers) before joining with the Kasai River.

LUNA (LOO-nah)   a) A people of Zaire that speak a Bantu language. b) (LOO-nuh) A mythological goddess of the moon. Also, the Spanish word for "moon" or "satellite" as well as the female name with the same meaning.

LUNDA (LOON-dah)   a) A Bantu people living in Shaba Province Zaire, Angola, and Zambia. b) From the seventeenth to nineteenth centuries A.D. the Kingdom of Lunda thrived in what is now southern Zaire.

LUSAKA (loo-SAH-kuh)   Zambia's capital since 1935 and main commercial center. The city was named after **LUSAAKAS**, a local chief. (Could be shortened to **LUSA**, which itself is the Finnish version of Elizabeth.)

LUWATA (loo-WAH-tah)   A name used to refer to the Berber people and their languages. There are some four million Luwata in Morocco and approximately three million in Algeria.

Male

LABAAN (leh-BAHN, leh-BAN)   A Somali male name.

LARBI (LAIR-bee)   Larbi Ben Barek was a Moroccan soccer player who played for France in the 1940s and 1950s.

LARI (LAH-ree)   A Congolese people who speak a Bantu language.

LAT (lah)   Lat Dior was a Wolof chief who became Damel (meaning king) of Cayor (now Senegal). He spearheaded the unsuccessful fight against French colonists in the late nineteenth century. Also, Lat a is short form of the English male name Latimer, which means "interpreter."

LATEEF (lah-TEEF)   Muslim male name that is popular in North Africa and means "pleasant, gentle." Yusef Lateef is a prominent jazz musician from Africa.

LE BARDO (leh BAHR-doh)   Also called **BARDAW** (BAHR-dah), this Tunisian town is found near Tunis, the country's capital.

LEBNA (LUHB-nuh)   Ethiopian male name meaning "heart"

or "soul." Lebna Dengel (DUHN-guhl, means "virgin") was Emperor of Abyssinia (present-day Ethiopia) from 1508–1540.

LEMA (LUH-mah)   Amharic of Ethiopia male name meaning "cultivated, developed."

LERIBE (leh-REE-bay)   A principal city in Lesotho.

LIBAN (LEE-bahn)   A town populated by Gabbra people in northern Kenya.

LIJ (luhj)   An Ethiopian honorary title or rank similar to the British title "Lord." Emperor Lij Iyasu (1896–1935), nephew of Menelik II, ruled Ethiopia from 1911 until 1916, at which time he was deposed by his aunt, Queen Zauditu.

LOBENGULA (loh-behn-GOO-luh)   A late nineteenth century king of the Matebele peoples of Zimbabwe. (Could be shortened to **BEN**.)

LUCALA (loo-KAH-luh)   A chief of the Ndongo Kingdom of Angola in the seventeenth century. (Could be shortened to **LU**.)

LUKI (LOO-kee)   In West Africa this is a popular short form of the name **LUQMAN** (see below.)

LUMUMBA (loo-MOOM-bah)   A Congolese name meaning "gifted."

LUQMAN (LOOK-man, look-MAHN)   Male name which is popular among West and North African Muslims. Luqman was an Islamic philosopher.

LUSAAKAS (loo-SAHK-uhs)   See LUSAKA under female.

LUSALA (loo-SAH-lah)   A Luhya of Kenya male name meaning "whip."

LUSHANGE (loo-SHAHN-gay)   A people of Zambia who speak a Bantu language.

LUTHULI (loo-TOO-lee, loo-THOO-lee)   A Zulu name. Chief Albert John Luthuli (1898–1968) of the Amakholwa Zulu peoples was a former president of the African National Congress, a South African political organization opposed to apartheid. He was the first African to win the Nobel Peace Prize in 1960, and he wrote the book *Let My People Go* in 1962.

LUXOR (LOOK-sawr, LUK-sor)   A city in southern Egypt on the east banks of the Nile. As the ancient city of Thebes, it was Egypt's southern pharoanic capital. Luxor's temple ruins and monuments, including the Temple of Amon, Temple of Karnak, and Valley of the Kings, make it a major tourist attraction. Its name is of Arabic origin and means "the palaces."

M

Justice is like fire, even if you cover it with a veil, it still burns.

—Proverb from Madagascar

Female

MADA (MAH-dah) A people living in Benue-Plateau State, Nigeria. A separate group of Mada people live in Cameroon. Also, Mada is the diminutive form of the Hebrew female name Magdalene, which means "high tower."

MAGADI (mah-GAHD-ee) Lake Magadi, located southwest of Nairobi, Kenya, is one of the hottest spots on the floor of the Rift Valley and a favorite site for ornithologists. It is 12.5 miles (20 kilometers) long and is filled with Trona deposits, which are used to make Soda Ash. "Magadi" is the Kiswahili word for "soda."

MAGDA (MAHG-duh) A short form of the Hebrew female name Magdalene, which means "high tower" and is believed by some to refer to the former Abyssinian (Ethiopian) acropolis of Magdala.

MAGDALA (MAG-duh-luh) A 1,000-foot-high town in Ethiopia's central highlands. In the mid-1800s, under Emperor Theodore II, Magdala was a mountain fortress and the main capital of Abyssinia (present-day Ethiopia).

MAISHA (mah-EE-shah) Kiswahili word meaning "life."

MAKDA (MAHK-duh) Ethiopian version of the Hebrew female name MAGDA (see above), which means "high tower" or "woman of Magdala."

MAKEBA (mah-KAY-bah)   Miriam Makeba is a South African vocalist who was exiled from her homeland in 1960. She earned the titles "Mama Africa" and "Empress of African Song" for combining traditional and modern African music in her songs. She was formerly married to South African trumpeter Hugh Masekela and American civil rights activist Stokely Carmichael. Her exile ended in 1991.

MAKEDA (mah-KUH-dah)   Amharic of Ethiopia female name meaning "beautiful armrest" referring to traditional carved wood armrests. Makeda was the name of the Queen of Sheba.

MAKEMBA (mah-KAYM-bah)   Central African female name referring to a Congolese goddess.

MAKENA (mah-KAY-nuh)   A Kikuyu of Kenya female name meaning "the happy one."

MALAIKA (mah-LAH-EE-kah, mah-LIGH-kuh)   Kiswahili word for "angel." Malaika is the title of a popular East African song.

MALANGE (muh-LAN-juh)   The capital city of Malange District in northern Angola and the regional agricultural market town.

MALI (MAH-lee)   a) Mali was an ancient empire in the savannah lands of West Africa, in what are now the countries of Mali, Senegal, and Gambia. The empire gained its wealth from locally mined gold and from dominating trade in the area. The name Mali is derived either from the word in the Bambara language for rhinoceros or from the name of the Malinke (also called Mandingo) peoples. b) A Kiswahili word meaning "wealth, riches." c) A Thai name for females meaning "jasmine flower."

MALINDI (muh-LIN-dee)   Also spelled **MELINDA** and **MELINDE**, this coastal Kenyan resort town with a small port is popular with tourists for game fishing and water sports. In the sixteenth century Malindi was an important Swahili port that rivaled Mombasa, a large port further south. The town was named by Portuguese explorer Vasco de Gama after his wife.

MALKIA (MAHL-kee-ah) A Kiswahili word meaning "queen." It is related to the Muslim female name **MALIKA** and Hebrew female name **MALKA** (MAHL-kah) which also mean "queen."

MANDA (MAN-duh) a) Manda Island off Kenya's east coast was a hub of old Swahili culture and is now an important archaeological site with ruins dating from the fourteenth and fifteenth centuries. b) A town in southern Tanzania on the shores of Lake Nyasa. c) Manda National Park is a wildlife refuge in Chad that was opened in 1965. d) A Hausa word for medicinal salts. e) Short form of the Spanish name Armanda, which means "woman of battle."

MANDARA (mahn-DAHR-ah) a) A people living in the Bornu Region of Nigeria and in Cameroon who speak a Chadic language. b) The Mandara Mountains are found in northern Cameroon and are home to the Kirdi people. c) (mahn-DAH-rah) According to Hindu mythology, the name of a tree under which one can sit and their cares will disappear.

MANDERA (man-DAIR-uh) A town in Kenya near the border with Somalia and Ethiopia.

MANDISA (mahn-DEE-sah) Xhosa of South Africa female name meaning "sweet."

MANYARA (muhn-YAHR-uh) A lake and national park in northeastern Tanzania.

MANYIKA (mah-NYEE-kah) A people living in Mozambique and Zimbabwe. They speak a Bantu language also called Manyika.

MAPENZI (mah-PEHN-zee) or **MPENZI** (mPEHN-zee) A Swahili female name meaning "beloved." In Tonga language of Zambia and Zimbabwe "mapenzi" means "suffering."

MARA (MAH-ruh) a) A Kiswahili word meaning "a time." For instance, "mara moja" means "one time." b) A river flowing through Kenya and Tanzania and into Lake Victoria. c) A Hebrew female name that means "sea of bitterness."

MARAHABA (MAH-rah-HAH-bah) A Kiswahili word for "thank you."

MARGAI Sir Milton Margai (1895–1964) was the first prime minister of Sierra Leone from 1961–1964. His brother, Sir Albert Michael Margai, succeeded him as prime minister from 1964–1967.

MARGI (MAHR-gee) A people of Cameroon and Nigeria who speak a Chadic language.

MARI (MAH-ree) Also spelled **MHARI**, a people of Zimbabwe who speak a dialect of Karanga. Mari is also a contemporary spelling of the female name Mary.

MARIAMA (mah-ree-AHM-ah) A female name popular in West Africa meaning "gift of God." Mariama Ba is a Senegalese writer concentrating on Muslim womens' issues. Her works include *Scarlet Song* and *So Long A Letter*.

MARJANI (mahr-JAH-nee) Swahili female name meaning "coral" derived from the Kiswahili word for "red coral," **MARIJANI** (MAH-ree-JAH-nee).

MAROUA (muh-ROO-uh) A town in northern Cameroon.

MARWE (MAHR-way) Chaga of Tanzania female name.

MASHASHA (muh-SHAH-shah) A people of Zambia who speak a Bantu language. (Could be shortened to **MASHA**, itself a Russian female name meaning "bitter" or "flower.")

MASINDI (muh-SIN-dee) A town in west-central Uganda.

MASINISSA (ma-si-NI-suh) From around 238–149 B.C. Masinissa was the first king of Numidia, an ancient North African state.

MASSASSI (muh-SAHS-see) According to Makoni of Zimbabwe legend, Massassi was the first female on earth, equivalent to the biblical Eve.

MAWUNYAGA (MAH-woo-NYAH-gah) An Ewe of Ghana name meaning "God is great."

MAVIHA (mah-VEE-hah) A people of Mozambique who speak a Bantu language.

MEDEA (mi-DEE-uh) In Greek mythology, this African princess and daughter of King Aeetes was known for her skills in sorcery. Her name means "cunning."

MEMA (MAY-mah)   Kiswahili word meaning "good things."

MERCA (MAIR-kuh)   A city on the Indian Ocean coast in southern Somalia within a major agricultural region.

MERINA (MAIR-i-nuh, MAIR-nuh)   Also called **IMERINA** (i-MAIR-i-nuh) and **ANTIMERINA** (ahn-ti-MAIR-nuh), over one million Merina people live in the central province of Madagascar. They constitute about 25 percent of the country's population. The Merina are descendants of Indonesian settlers who probably arrived in outrigger canoes before A.D. 700. They speak Malagasy, which is related to Indonesian languages and in which extensive literature is written. The name Merina means "people of the highlands."

MIHAVANI (mee-hah-VAH-nee)   A people from Mozambique.

MIMI (MEE-mee)   a) The Kiswahili word for "I, me, myself." b) A people living in the Wadai region of Chad. Their language belongs to an isolated language group. c) Also, a French name that means "martial, strong."

MINNA (MIN-uh)   a) A Gruma of West Africa word meaning "mother." b) A town in northern Nigeria that is the home of novelist Cyprian Ekwensi. c) Also, a short form of the German female name Wilhelmina, which means "warrior, guardian."

MINYA (MIN-yuh)   a) A city in northern Egypt on the Nile River. b) A people in Cote D'Ivoire who speak a language related to Malinke. c) Also called the **MINYANKA**, a people who are a subgroup of the Senufo people of Mali. d) Pronounced MEEN-yah, it is a Kiswahili word meaning "to squeeze out." e) Also, a Native American female name meaning "big sister."

MIRIAM (MAIR-ee-uhm)   Muslim female name that is very popular in Ethiopia and Somalia. Miriam refers to the biblical Mary.

MISRAK (MUHS-rahk)   Amharic and Tigrinya of Ethiopia female name meaning "east."

MOENA (moh-AY-nuh)   Moena Monenga is a legendary woman chief from Central Africa who, because of her anger at villagers who denied her food and shelter, caused the offending village to sink into a hole that proceeded to fill up with water. This is the mythological origin of Lake Dilolo, located in Zaire on the border with Angola.

MONA (MOH-nah)   a) A language spoken in southern Togo. b) A Muslim female name meaning "hope." c) Swaziland male name meaning "jealous." d) European female name meaning "noble lady."

MONICA (MON-i-kuh)   A Catholic saint born in North Africa at Tagaste (present-day Algeria) around 323 A.D. Monica died in Italy in 387 A.D. while preparing to return to Africa. She was the mother of Saint Augustine, who wrote a biography of his mother called *Confessions*. Monica, whose feast day is August 27, is the patron saint of married women. The name Monica is of Latin origin and means "counselor," although some believe Monica is a Berber name derived from the name of the Libyan goddess **MON** (mon).

MONIFA (moh-NEE-fah)   Yoruba of Nigeria female name meaning "I am lucky."

MUJAJI (moo-JAH-jee)   Mujaji II, according to South African legend, is the Rain Queen who never dies.

MUMBI (MOOM-bee)   Also spelled **MOOMBI**, this Kikuyu of Kenya female name refers to the legendary wife of Gikuyu, the founder of the Kikuyu people. Mumbi and Gikuyu's nine daughters grew into the nine clans of the Kikuyu, each carrying the name of one of the daughters. Also, Mumbi is the Akamba of Kenya name for their supreme god and means "fashioner."

MUTHONI (moo-THOH-nee)   Traditionally, the Kikuyu of Kenya used this name to address female in-laws. Now it is a common female name in Kenya. It is pronounced with a hard "th" as in "the," as opposed to the soft "th" of "therapy."

MACHUPA (mah-CHOO-pah)   Swahili male name meaning "one who enjoys drinking," probably derived from the Kiswahili word "chupa" that means "bottle."

MADING (mah-DING)   A male name of the Dinka of South Sudan. Francis Mading Deng was born in 1938 in South Sudan. He was the son of a paramount chief of the Ngok Dinka peoples. Mading earned degrees from Khartoum University and Yale University. He went on to teach law at New York University and Columbia Law School. He served as Sudan's ambassador to the Scandinavian countries, the United States, and Canada. Mading has written numerous scholarly books about his people, the Dinka of South Sudan. As an infant he was bestowed the name Mading after a bull that had been slaughtered at his mother's wedding.

MAHMOUD (MAH-mood)   Muslim male name meaning "fulfillment" which is popular in North Africa.

MALAKAL (MAHL-uh-kahl)   A town on the White Nile in southeastern Sudan.

MALIK (MA-lik)   This Muslim male name meaning "king" is popular among the Wolof of Senegal.

MALINKE (muh-LING-kee)   Also called **MANDINGO,** a people and their language found in Mali, Senegal, Guinea-Bissau, Cote D'Ivoire, and Guinea. American author Alex Haley traced his ancestors to a Malinke village in The Gambia called Juffure. (Could be shortened to **LINK.**)

MAMO (MAH-moh)   Amharic of Ethiopia male name often used to address a little boy whose name is unknown. Mamo Wolde is an Ethiopian who won a gold medal in the 1968 Olympics for the marathon with a time of 2:20:26.4. Also, Mamo is a Hawaiian name for males and females meaning "yellow bird" or "saffron flower."

MANAS (MAHN-uhs)   Manas Buthelezi is a Lutheran bishop and leader of the South African Council of Churches. He espouses what is called the "theology of the oppressed."

MANDELA (mahn-DEHL-ah)   Nelson Rolihlahla Mandela was born in 1918 in Transkei, South Africa, to a tribal chief. He became a lawyer and helped organize the African National Congress (ANC), the chief opposition group to white minority rule in South Africa, of which he later became president. In 1964 Mandela was sentenced to life in prison on Robben Island for his anti-apartheid activities. He was finally released in 1990. Mandela's speeches and writings are collected in the book *No Easy Walk to Freedom*.

MANI (MAH-nee)   A title meaning "lord" or "king" formerly used in central Africa. It is also a Congolese male name meaning "from the mountain."

MANSA a) (MAHN-sah)   This Mande word meaning "sultan" was used as a title for Malian kings. Mansa Musa ruled the Mali Empire from A.D. 1312–1332. Under his control the empire reached from the Atlantic Ocean to Nigeria. Its capital city was Niani, and the cities of Djenne and Timbuktu gained status as world-class Islamic academic and cultural centers. Mansa Musa is famous for his legendary pilgrimage to Mecca; as he passed through Egypt he handed out so much gold that the local economy collapsed. b) (MAHN-suh)   A town in northern Zambia.

MANU (mah-NOO)   Akan of Ghana name used for second-born children. Manu Dibango is a Cameroonian musician whose musical style, as well as the name of his biggest hit single, is called "Soul Makossa."

MANUTE (muh-NOOT)   A Dinka of South Sudan male name. Manute Bol, a Dinka, is a professional basketball player in the NBA in the United States.

MANZINI (MAHN-zee-nee)   A town in central Swaziland that was formerly the country's capital.

MAPUTO (muh-POO-toh)   Maputo was the son of Nuagobe, a Mozambican chief in the eighteenth century. The Maputo River was named after him and later the capital city of Mozambique took its name from this river.

MARKOS (MAHR-kohs)   Ethiopian male name referring to the biblical disciple Mark. Mark is of Latin origin and means "warlike." The Italian version of the name is MARCO and the German version is MARKOS.

MARTI (MAHR-tee)   A small town north of the town of Maralal in the Rift Valley Province of Kenya. This town is in a hot, arid region known as Samburuland.

MASA (mah-SAH)   A people from Chad and Cameroon. The Masa speak a Chado-Hamitic language.

MASAKIN (mah-sah-KEEN)   A people of the Sudan from the Nubian ethnic group who speak a Koalib-Tagoi language. Traditionally they are cattle-raisers and for recreation they engage in the sport of wrestling. Another spelling of their name is **MESAKIN** (may-sah-KEEN), which is a word meaning "poor people."

MASEKELA (mah-seh-KAY-lah)   Hugh Masekela is a South African jazz trumpeter. He wrote the 1960s pop hit "Up, Up, and Away." Masekela was formerly married to Miriam Makeba.

MASILO (mah-SEE-loh)   A Setswana of Botswana male name.

MASKINI (mah-SKEE-nee)   A Swahili male name and Kiswahili word meaning "poor."

MASSAWA (mah-SAH-wah)   An important port town on the Red Sea in Eritrea (contested former province of northern Ethiopia). This town is built on a coral island and has an extremely hot climate. The name means "to shout" in a local language.

MASUD (mah-SOOD)   Also spelled **MASOUD**, this Swahili and Muslim male name means "fortunate, happy."

MATATA (mah-TAH-tah)   A Swahili male name meaning "troublemaker." "Hakuna (hah-KOO-nah) Matata" is a popular expression among tourists and locals of East Africa; it means "no problem."

MATHANI (mah-THAH-nee)   A popular name of the Kikuyu people of Kenya which means "commandments."

MATUNDE (mah-TOON-day)   A Luya of Kenya male name meaning "fruits," probably derived from the Kiswahili word "matunda" with the same meaning.

MAURICE (mohr-EES)   This legendary Christian soldier came from the island of Mauritius. He served as captain of the Roman army's Theban Legion. He is the patron saint of armies whose feast day is celebrated in Austria on September 22. His name means "Moorish, dark-skinned."

MEJA (MAY-jah)   Meja Mwangi is a Kenyan novelist whose work *Going Down River Road* recalls the rough life of an urban laborer. Meja is the Kiswahili word meaning "major" as derived from English; it is not a traditional name.

MEKONNEN (meh-koh-NUHN)   Amharic and Tigrinya of Ethiopia male name meaning "respected, elite."

MELAKU (meh-LAH-koo)   Amharic of Ethiopia male name meaning "the angel."

MELFI (MEHL-fee)   A town in southern Chad.

MELESSE (muh-LUH-suh)   Amharic and Tigrinya of Ethiopia name meaning "he has returned (something)."

MEMNON (MEHM-non)   According to ancient Greek mythology, Memnon was an Aethiopian (meaning black African) king who led his African troops to Troy to assist the Trojans. In the ensuing battle he slayed Antilochus, but he himself was killed by Achilles. The gods converted his remaining troops into birds, and they flew away from the battlefield. Memnon was the son of Tithonus and Eos (also known as Aurora).

MEMPHIS (MEHM-fuhs)   The pharonic capital of ancient Lower Egypt from 2600–2190 B.C. Located on the west banks of the Nile River not far from Cairo, Memphis's ancient temples and ruins make it a modern-day tourist attraction. The name comes from ancient Egyptian and means either "the beautiful site" or "the place of the Phtah."

MENELIK (MEHN-uh-lik, min-ee-LIK)   Amharic of Ethiopia male name meaning "son of the wise man" or "what will he send?" Menelik I, son of the Queen of Sheba and King Solomon of Jerusalem, ruled Abyssinia (Ethiopia) in the tenth century B.C. Menelik II, Emperor of Ethiopia from 1889 until his death in 1913, also claimed to be a descendent of Solomon and Sheba.

MENGISTU (mehn-GI-stoo)   Mengistu Haile-Mariam was the Marxist ruler of Ethiopia from 1974 until 1991. His full name means "government by the power of Mary."

MENSAH (MEHN-sah)   Ewe of Ghana name for third-born males.

MERCURIUS (mur-kyur-EE-oos)   A Greek name meaning "Mercury." Mercurius was emperor of the Christian Kingdom of Nobatia, in present-day Sudan. Mercurius succeeded in uniting the three Christian Nubian Kingdoms of Nobatia, Makurrah, and Alwah around A.D. 710, creating a united territory stretching from the Nile River valley at Aswan south into Sudan and east to the Ethiopian border.

MERILLE (muh-RI-lay)   A people living in Ethiopia around the northern shores of Lake Turkana. Also called the **GELABA** (guh-LAHB-ah), they speak a Cushitic language.

MEROË (MEHR-uh-wee)   From the fourth century B.C. through A.D. 350, this city served as the capital for Aethiopian (meaning black African) kings and queens of the ancient kingdoms of Kush and Meroë. Meroë was situated between the Atbara and Nile rivers of Sudan, near the town of Shendy. A Meroitic alphabet and script were invented. The ruins of this city are impressive and include palaces and pyramids. Slaves with black skin in Greco-Roman societies were sometimes given the name Meroë, referring to their assumed origin in the kingdom of Kush.

MIKEA (mi-KAY-ah)   A clan of the Saklava ethnic group of Madagascar. Although Saklava means "people of the long valleys," the Mikea are primarily forest dwellers whose survival skills are compared to those of the Bushmen of the Kalahari. The Mikea are also called the **VAZIMBA** (vah-ZEEM-bah).

MILTIADES (mil-TIGH-uh-deez)   Believed to be an African, Miltiades became pope in A.D. 311 and died shortly thereafter in A.D. 314. Also called **MELCHIADES** (mehl-KIGH-uh-deez), he is a Catholic saint whose feast day is December 10. (Could be shortened to **MEL, MILT,** or **TI.**)

MIN (min) Min is believed to be the first ruler of Egypt.

MIRUTS (muh-ROOTS) Tigrinya of Ethiopia male name meaning "he who has been chosen." Miruts Yifter, an Ethiopian, won two Olympic gold medals in 1980 for the 5,000-meter run with a time of 13:21.0 and for the 10,000-meter run with a time of 27:42.7.

MOGO (MOH-goh) Mogo wa Kebiro was a Kikuyu of Kenya mystic who prophesied the coming of white colonialists.

MOKTAR (MOHK-tahr) Also spelled **MUKHTAR** (MOOK-tahr), a Muslim male name meaning "chosen." Moktar Ould Daddah was the first president of independent Mauritania. He was chairman of the Organization for African Unity (OAU) from 1971–1972. (Could be shortened to **MOKE**.)

MOLIMO (moh-LEE-moh) The deity of the forest, according to the Mbuti pygmies of the Ituri forest of northeast Zaire. Also, a Native American male name meaning "the bear enters the tree's shade." (Could be shortened to **MO**, itself an Efik of Nigeria word for "water.")

MONGO (MOHN-goh) A Yoruba of Nigeria male name meaning "famous." Mongo Beti is the pen name of Alexandre Biyidi from Cameroon. Books by Beti include *Mission to Kala* and *The Poor Christ of Bomba*.

MONGO-MA-LOBA (MOHN-goh-mah-LOH-bah) The local name for Mount Cameroon's highest peak, the Great Cameroon. It means "throne of thunder."

MONROVIA (muhn-ROH-vee-uh) The capital city of Liberia, which was established for resettlement of freed North American slaves. Originally called Cristopolis, it was renamed Monrovia after United States president James Monroe in 1822 by the American Colonization Society. (Could be shortened to **MONROE**, itself an Irish surname meaning "red bog" or "of the mouth of the Roe River.")

MONYYAK (mohn-YAHK) A Dinka of southern Sudan male name meaning "man of the drought."

MORENIKE (mohr-ay-NEE-kay) Nigerian male name meaning "good luck."

MORI (MOHR-ee)   Ugandan male name for sons born before the loan on the wife's dowry has been paid off.

MORY (MOR-ee)   Mory Kante is a Guinean griot (traditional West African musician/historian/storyteller) whose international popularity has earned him the title, the "Mandingo Lion."

MOSES (MOH-ziz, MOH-zis)   Abba Moses, known as the "Father of the Desert of Scetis," was a tall African monk in fourth-century Roman-Egypt. He was revered for his humility and Christian virtues. It was well-known that he was a former slave, thief, and, some say, murderer. Moses is a male name referring to the biblical Moses who led the Israelites out of Egypt where they had been enslaved. The name is either of Hebrew origin meaning "saved from water," or Egyptian origin meaning "child, son."

MOSHI (MOH-shee)   a) A city in northeast Tanzania on the southern slopes of Mount Kilimanjaro. Moshi is an economic and educational hub for East Africa. b) A Kiswahili word meaning "smoke."

MOSHOESHOE (moh-SHWAY-shway)   A male Sesotho name and the name of two kings of the Lesotho kingdom.

MOSI (MOH-see)   a) A Swahili name for firstborn children. b) A Kiswahili word meaning "one." c) In Zambia the word "mosi" means "smoke" and is found in the local name for Victoria Falls, Mosiatunya (also Musi-o-Tunya), meaning "the smoke that thunders."

MOYO (MOH-yoh)   a) A Zezuru of Zimbabwe male name meaning "heart." b) The Kiswahili word for "heart." c) A town in northern Uganda.

MTOTO (m-TOH-toh)   Kiswahili word for "child, kid." It is an affectionate name used for children.

MUENDA (moo-AYN-duh)   A Meru of Kenya male name meaning "one who cares for others."

MUHAMMED (moo-HAM-id)   or **MOHAMMED** (moh-HAM-id) This name of the Muslim prophet Muhammed is very popular in North Africa. It means "the praised one." a) Muhammed Toure ruled the West African kingdom of Songhai for thirty years following Sunni Ali's sudden death in 1492. b) Muhammed Bello was a lieutenant to Uthman dan Fodio. He helped establish peace after Uthman's holy war, which created the empire of Sokoto in today's northern Nigeria.

MUREITHI (moor-AYEE-thee)   Kikuyu of Kenya male name meaning "herdsman, shepherd."

MURLE (MOOR-lee)   Also called the **BEIR**, the Murle are a people of southern Sudan. They speak a Didinga-Murle language.

MUSA (MOO-sah)   Popular among the Wolof of Senegal, this Muslim and Swahili male name means "mercy" or "saved from the water" and refers to the biblical Moses.

MUTESA (moo-TEH-suh)   King Frederick Mutesa III was the last of the kings, called "kabakas," of the Buganda kingdom of Uganda. He became the first president of Uganda from independence in 1962 until he was deposed in 1966. He was nicknamed King Freddie by the Ugandan people.

MWAKA (MWAH-kah)   A Buganda of Uganda name for children born on New Year's Eve. Mwaka is the Kiswahili word for "year."

MWINYI (m-WEEN-yee)   Swahili male name meaning "lord, master, king." Ali Hassan Mwinyi became the second president of Tanzania in 1985, succeeding Julius K. Nyerere.

MWITA (m-WEE-tah)   Swahili male name and Kiswahili word meaning "the one who is calling."

N

When the mouse laughs at the cat there is a hole nearby.

—Nigerian proverb

Female

NABILA (nah-BEE-lah) Also spelled **NABEELA**, this Muslim female name is popular in Egypt. It means "noble."

NADIA (NA-dee-uh, NAH-dee-uh) A Muslim female name popular in the Sudan that means "full of dew." Nadia is also a version of the Eastern European name Nadine, which means "hope."

NADIFA (nah-DEEF-ah) Somali female name meaning "born between two seasons."

NADRA (NAH-drah) Kiswahili word meaning "unusual." From the same root word as the Muslim female name **NADIRA** (nah-DEER-ah), which means "rare."

NAFANA Also called the **NFANTRA**, these are a people of Burkina Faso who speak Senufo.

NAIVASHA (nigh-VAHSH-uh) Lake Naivasha is located in the Rift Valley in Kenya. The lake's abundant bird life, fish, and hippopotami attracts tourists and naturalists from around the world. In the middle of Lake Naivasha is Crescent Island, a bird sanctuary. The lake is also unique in that it is believed not to have an outlet.

NAJA (NAH-jah) A Muslim female name that is popular in Somalia and means "success."

NAJACA (nah-JAH-kah) A rural village in Mozambique.

NAJJA (NAHJ-jah)   Baganda of Uganda name for second-born children.

NAKI (NAH-kee)   An Adangbe of Ghana name for the first girl in the family.

NALIAKA (nah-lee-AH-kah)   Luya of western Kenya female name meaning "wedding."

NALONGO (nah-LOHN-goh)   According to Baganda of Uganda tradition, when a woman has twins she gives herself this name.

NANA (nah-NAH)   Ghanaian female name meaning "mother of the Earth." Also, a Krobo and Akan of Ghana title for "chief or queen mother."

NANDE (NAHN-day)   The mother of Chaka Zulu. Because of her fiery temper, Nande was banned from her husband's court.

NANDI (NAN-dee)   A people living in western Kenya who speak a language of the same name, which is a Nilo-Hamitic language of the Kalenjin group.

NANGILA (nahn-GEE-lah)   A Luya of Kenya name for children born while the parents were travelling.

NANTALE (nahn-TAHL-ay)   A Baganda of Uganda female name for those whose clan totem is a lion.

NATA (NAH-tah)   a) A people of northern Tanzania who speak a Bantu language. b) A Kiswahili word that means "to adhere, be sticky, be faithful." c) A Hausa of Nigeria word for "mother." d) A town in northern Botswana. e) A female name used in India meaning "rope dancer." f) A short form of the name Natalie, of Latin origin and meaning "born at Christmas time."

NAWAL (nah-WAHL)   Muslim female name popular in North Africa that means "gift, attainment." Nawal el Moutawakel of Morocco won the Olympic gold medal in 1984 for women's 400-meter hurdles with a time of 54.61. Nawal al-Sa'Dawi is an Egyptian physician and feminist writer.

NAZI (NAH-zee)   A female name of the Giriami people of coastal Kenya meaning "coconut." It is also a Kiswahili word with the same meaning. (Readers should note that this name could easily be mistaken for Nazi (NAHT-see), referring to the former fascist political party of Germany.)

NDILA (n-DEE-lah)   A Kamba of Kenya unisex name meaning "billy goat."

NDOLA (n-DOH-luh)   A city of about one-half million people in northern Zambia's copperbelt region.

NEEMA (nay-AY-mah)   A Swahili female name meaning "born at a prosperous time." The name is derived from the Kiswahili word "neemeka" (nay-ay-MAY-kah) meaning "to be well off." Also, the Kiswahili word "neema" means "grace of God, favor."

NEFERTITI (NEHF-uhr-TEE-tee)   An Egyptian female name meaning "the beautiful one has arrived." Nefertiti was an Egyptian queen and the wife of Akhenaten in the fourteenth century B.C.

NEHANDA (neh-HAHN-dah)   A Zezuru of Zimbabwe female name meaning "hardiness." Nehanda Nyagasikan was a heroine and priestess of the Shona people of Zimbabwe who was worshipped in ancient times.

NELION   Named after a Masai chief, Nelion is one of the peaks of Mount Kenya. Nelion stands 17,022 feet (5,188 meters) high.

NENA (NAY-nah)   The Kiswahili word meaning "speak."

NENET (NEH-neht)   An Egyptian mythological goddess who signifies still waters, stillness.

NIA (NEE-ah)   A Kiswahili word meaning "resolve, purpose."

NIA NIA (NEE-uh NEE-uh)   A town in Zaire near the Ugandan border.

NIANI (nee-ah-NEE)   The ancient capital of the kingdom of Mali. Niani is located near the modern city of Bamako, Mali. The ancient kingdom of Mali was so immense, it took three months to cross on pack animals.

NIGESA (nee-GAY-sah)   Lumasada of Kenya female name for children born in the harvest season. Spelled **NAGESA** (nah-GAY-sah) it is a Lugisu of Uganda name with the same meaning.

NIKKI (NIK-ee)   A town in northeastern Benin.

NINI (NEE-nee)   West African female name meaning "stone."

NISHAN (NEE-shahn)   Amharic of Ethiopia female name meaning "award, medal." LISHAN is an Ethiopian name with the same meaning.

NJEMILE (n-jeh-MEE-lay)   Ngoni of Malawi female name that means "upstanding."

NKECHI (n-KAY-kee)   Nigerian female name meaning "loyal."

NNAMBI (n-NAHM-bee)   According to Baganda of Uganda legend, Kintu and Nnambi were the original couple of mankind, equivalent to the biblical Adam and Eve.

NOLA (NOH-luh)   a) A river town in western Central African Republic. b) A female name of Latin origin meaning "olive."

NONI (NOH-nee)   The short form of the Kikuyu of Kenya female name MUTHONI. Noni Jabavu is the author of the novel, *The Ochre People,* in which she talks about the life of the Xhosa people of South Africa. Her father is a prominent Xhosa journalist and politician.

NUPE (NOO-pay)   A people of Nigeria as well as the name of their former Hausa kingdom of the sixteenth to nineteenth centuries in what is now Nigeria.

NURU (NOO-roo)   Swahili female and male name meaning "light" or "born during the day." Related to the Muslim female name **NUR** (noor), which means "light."

NYALA (nee-YAH-lah)   The name of a rare mountain goat found only in Ethiopia.

NYANDA (nee-AN-duh)   A town in Zimbabwe near the Zimbabwe ruins.

NYLA (NIGH-luh)   An Egyptian female name and the name of a princess of ancient Egypt.

NYOKABI (nyoh-KAHB-ee)   Kenyan name for females of mixed Kikuyu and Masai blood.

NYIKA (NYEE-kuh)   a) A people living in coastal areas of Kenya and Tanzania and who speak a Bantu language. b) The Kiswahili word for "dry grasslands, scrub-land, wilderness."

98

c) Nyika Park is a game park in northern Malawi. d) A local name for water chestnuts in Tanzania.

NZINGA (n-ZING-uh)   The name of various Congolese monarchs. It means "from the river." Nzinga Mbandi (1583–1663) was queen of both the Ndongo and Matamba kingdoms in present-day Angola. Queen Nzinga organized strong military resistance against Portuguese settlers.

Male

NADIF (nah-DEEF)   A Somali male name meaning "born between two seasons."

NADIR (nah-DEER)   A Muslim male name popular in the Sudan that means "precious, rare."

NAKURU (nah-KOO-roo)   The provincial capital of the Rift Valley Province of Kenya. Located in the highlands, it is the main commercial center for farmers of the area. The city overlooks Lake Nakuru, where millions of flamingos gather, turning the shoreline a pink hue.

NASSER (NAS-uhr)   a) Lake Nasser is an artificial lake formed by the Aswan High Dam on the Nile River. The lake is located in both Egypt and Sudan. It is three-hundred-miles (480 kilometers) long and thirty miles (48 kilometers) at its widest point. b) Gamal Abdel Nasser (1918–1970) was president of Egypt from 1954–1970, when he died of a heart attack. His presidency is said to have ushered Egypt into a prominent position in both world and inter-Arab politics. c) Nasser is an Arabic male name meaning "victorious."

NASSOR (NAH-sohr)   The Swahili variation of the Arabic name Nasser, which means "victorious."

NATAL (nuh-TAHL)   A province of South Africa so named because it was first sighted by Portuguese explorers on Christmas day in 1497. Natale is the Portuguese word for Christmas.

NATRON (NAY-tron, NAY-truhn)   Lake Natron is found in Tanzania in the Rift Valley system. Natron refers to the lake's content of sodium bicarbonate. The lake covers about 220 square miles (563 kilometers). (Could be shortened to **NATE**.)

NAZARET (nahz-RAYT, nah-suh-RAHT) A town in Ethiopia named after the city of Nazareth in Palestine (Israel).

NDUGU (n-DOO-goo) A Kiswahili word meaning "kinsman, brother."

NDULU (n-DOO-loo) An Ibo of Nigeria male name meaning "dove."

NEGASH (NUH-gahsh) Amharic and Tigrinya of Ethiopia male name meaning "he is bound to be king, he is next in line for the throne."

NEGASI (nuh-GAH-see) Amharic and Tigrinya of Ethiopia male name meaning "he will be crowned."

NEGUS (NUH-goos, NEE-guhs, ni-GOOS) In northern Ethiopia this male name and royal title means "king, emperor."

NEILOS (NIGH-lohs) An early Greek name for the Nile River.

NGOLA (n-GOH-luh) A title used for early monarchs of Angola and the root of the country's name.

NGWEE (n-GWAY) The name of this Zambian unit of currency means "sunray."

NIAMEY (nyah-MAY, nee-AH-may) The capital city of Niger since 1927. (The former capital was Zinder.) Niamey is located on the northern bank of the Niger River.

NICAEUS (NIK-ee-uhs) Pliny the Elder, a scholar of ancient Rome, wrote about this famous Aethiopian (meaning African) boxer. Nicaeus was born in Byzantium of a white mother and Aethiopian father.

NICANDER (ni-KAN-dur, nigh-KAN-dur) An Egyptian doctor who was killed in A.D. 304 for treating Christian prisoners. He is a Catholic saint whose feast day is March 15.

NICO (NEE-koh) Prince Nico Mbarga, Cameroonian by birth but raised in Nigeria, is a musician whose particular style of juju music is called Panco Highlife. Nico's biggest hit was his album "Sweet Mother," released in 1976.

NILE (nighl) The Nile is the longest river in Africa and the largest in the world. It is 4,187 miles (6,699 kilometers) long, covering one-tenth of Africa's land surface. Over fifty million people live in the Nile basin area. The Blue Nile begins its course in Ethiopia, and the White Nile begins in Uganda. They converge in Khartoum, Sudan, and run north to Alexandria, Egypt, where the Nile spills into the Mediterranean Sea.

NILUS (NIGH-lus) According to the ancient Greeks, Nilus was the god of the Nile River.

NJAU (n-JOW) A Kikuyu of Kenya male name meaning "young bull."

NKRUMAH (n-KROO-mah, n-KROO-muh) Also spelled **NKRUMA,** an Akan of Ghana male and female name for the ninth-born child. Kwame Nkrumah (1909–1972) was the first president of Ghana.

NYALI (NYAH-lee, nee-AH-lee) A people of eastern Zaire who speak a Bantu language. Also, Nyali Beach is found on Kenya's Indian Ocean coast.

NYASORE (nyah-SOHR-ay) A Kenyan name meaning "the thin one."

O

A good man will neither speak nor do as a bad man will; but if a man is bad, it makes no difference whether he be a black or white devil.

—From *Thoughts and Sentiments on the Evils of Slavery*, 1787, by Ottobah Cogoano, an anti-slavery activist in England of Ghanaian origin

Female

OBAX (OH-bah) A popular female name in Somalia that means "flower."

ODA (OH-duh) A town in southern Ghana. Also, a female European name meaning "rich."

OFRAH (OH-frah) A word for "moon" in Mandinka language of West Africa.

OLA (oh-LAH) An Ibo of Nigeria female name meaning "precious, worth," and a Yoruba of Nigeria male name meaning "wealth."

ONA (oh-NAH) An Iggara of West Africa word for "fire." Pronounced OH-nah, it is a female name derived from Latin meaning "the one, united."

ONAEDO (oh-nah-ay-DOH) An Ibo of Nigeria female name meaning "gold."

ONI (oh-NEE) West African female name meaning "desired." Pronounced AW-nee, it is a Yoruba of Nigeria female name meaning "born in a sacred location."

ONITSHA (oh-NICH-uh) An old city on the Niger River in Iboland in East-Central State, Nigeria. Onitsha is a commercial center with a huge market dominated by women traders who are referred to as the "merchant princesses of Onitsha."

ONYESHA (ohn-YAY-shah)   A Kiswahili word meaning "to show."

ORISA (or-i-SAH)   Also spelled **ORISHA,** the title for traditional spirits and gods of the Yoruba people of Nigeria.

OYOKO (oh-YOH-koh)   A clan of the Akan peoples of Ghana. Long ago these agricultural peoples were the core group that created the Ashanti peoples who settled around Kumasi, Ghana.

OZA (OH-zah)   A Betes people of western Cote D'Ivoire name meaning "the red." Also, a Kiswahili word meaning "to marry" (the act as performed by a priest).

OZORO (oh-ZOHR-oh)   Ozoro Esther was a beautiful prin cess and the daughter of King Tecla Haimanout of Abyssinia (now Ethiopia) in the eighteenth century. She married Ras Michael, a vizier (a high government official).

Male

OBA (OH-bah, AW-bah)   A title used in Benin and Nigeria meaning "king."

OBASI (oh-BAH-see)   Ibo of Nigeria male name meaning "in honor of the supreme God." Also, an Isubu of West Africa word for "good spirits."

OBI (OH-bee)   Common first name for males of the Ibo of Nigeria, meaning "heart."

OBIKE (oh-BEE-kay)   Ibo of Nigeria male name meaning "a strong household."

ODERO (oh-DAIR-oh)   A Luo of Kenya name meaning "granary" for those born during the harvest season.

ODILI (oh-DIL-ee)   The name of the narrator in the novel, *A Man of the People,* by Chinua Achebe.

ODION (oh-dee-OHN)   Nigerian male name for the first-born of twins.

OFFIN (oh-FEEN) This Ghanaian name refers to the Offin River. It is often used as a surname. The Europeanized version of the name is **FYNN** (feen).

OHINI (oh-HEEN-ee) Also spelled **OHENE,** this Akan of Ghana male name means "chief."

OJI (oh-JEE) Ibo of Nigeria male name meaning "bearer of gifts."

OJO (oh-JOH) Yoruba of Nigeria male name used when the birth was difficult. Also, the name of a people of Ghana.

OKELLO (oh-KEHL-oh) Ateso of Uganda name for a child born after twins.

OKO (oh-KOH) Adangbe of Ghana name for a male twin. Also, the word for "fire" in the Bonny language of Nigeria.

OKOTH (oh-KOHTH) Ugandan name meaning "born during the rains."

OKOT (oh-KOHT) Okot P'Bitek (1931–1982) is a Ugandan poet whose works include *Song of Lawino, Song of Ocol, The Hare and the Hornbill,* and *The Horn of My Love.*

OLORUN (oh-LOOR-oon) According to Yoruba of Nigeria mythology, Olorun is the god of creation and owner of the sky. The name means "owner."

OLYMPIUS (oh-LIMP-ee-uhs) A popular hero-athlete of the arena in Carthage, an ancient North African city-state, during the rule of the Vandals. Olympius, of African origin, had a physique like Hercules.

OMAR (OH-mahr) A Muslim male name popular in West Africa and Somalia meaning "most high" and referring to one of the Prophet Muhammed's followers. Omar Bongo became the second president of independent Gabon in 1967. He was born in 1935 in Lewai, Franceville, Gabon.

OMARI (oh-MAHR-ee) The Swahili variation of the name OMAR (see above).

OMDURMAN (OM-door-MAHN) Located on the White Nile River, this is the sister city of Khartoum, Sudan. Omdurman is an ancient city that houses the tomb of Mahdi and an Islamic college. (Could be shortened to **DURMAN.**)

ORAN (oh-RAHN) A province on Algeria's Mediterranean coast and a large city on the coast. The town's architecture displays Spanish and Arabic influences.

ORANMIYAN (oh-RAHN-mee-yahn) A prince of Ife who was summoned by the people of Benin to rule their empire in A.D. 1170.

OROMO (oh-ROHM-oh) The largest ethnic group in Ethiopia. Although they are often called **GALLA**—meaning "herdsmen"—by others, they call themselves Oromo, which means "the men." Some of the earliest converts to Christianity were Oromo, however there is also a large Oromo Muslim population. The Oromo are renowned for their skills in crafting silver beads.

OSIRIS (oh-SIGH-ris) This Egyptian god is the brother and husband of the goddess Isis. His annual death and rebirth symbolizes the continual rebirth of nature. According to the *Books of the Dead*, ancient Egyptian texts, Osiris was an African.

OTHIENO (oh-tee-EH-noh) Luo of Kenya male name meaning "born at night."

P and Q

However far the stream flows, it never forgets its source.

—Yoruba proverb

Female

PALASSA (pah-LAH-sah) A female name of African origin that was popular among African slaves in North America.

PANYA (PAHN-yah) Swahili female name and Kiswahili word meaning "mouse." Also, a Russian nickname for Stephania, a name of Greek origin which means "crowned one."

PASHA (PAH-shuh) The honorary title once placed after the names of African governors while North Africa was under Turkish rule. Emin Pasha was the German-born governor of Equatoria Province (now southern Sudan) who opposed slave trading. Although born Jewish, he adopted the Muslim name Emin. He was killed in 1892 on the Zaire River at Stanley Falls by slave traders. Also, "pasha" is a Kiswahili word meaning "cause to get." For example, "pasha moto" means "to warm up," or more literally, "to cause to get warmed up."

PENDA (PEHN-dah) A Swahili name meaning "beloved" and the Kiswahili word for "to love." For example, "nina kupenda" (NEE-nah koo-PEHN-dah) means "I love you."

PERSINNA (pur-SIN-uh) An Aethiopian (meaning black African) queen who, according to ancient Roman texts, gave birth to a white-skinned daughter.

PIA (PEE-yah) a) A Kiswahili word meaning "also" or "top" (as in a child's toy). b) A female name of Latin origin meaning "pious." c) A Hindi female name meaning "loved one."

PIANGA (pee-AHN-gah)   A people of Zaire with a population of a few thousand who speak a Bantu language.

PONI (POH-nee)   A Bari of South Sudan name for second-born females.

QALHATA (kahl-HAH-tah)   Known as "the mistress of Kush," this Nubian queen ruled Egypt after Taharqa under the XXV dynasty.

QATTARA (kah-TAHR-ah)   The Qattara Depression is a geological formation in northwest Egypt. This irregularly shaped depression in the Libyan Desert covers 10,000 square miles (25,900 square kilometers) and is the lowest spot in Egypt.

QENA (KAY-nuh)   A city on the Nile River in central Egypt with a population around 100,000. It is across the river from the ruins of the ancient city of Dendera.

QWARA (KWAHR-ah)   A people who live near Lake Tana in Ethiopia. The Qwara speak a Cushitic language.

Male

PAKI (PAH-kee)   Xhosa of South Africa male name meaning "witness."

PALIME (pah-LEE-may)   A town in southwestern Togo. Palime is the market center of an important agricultural region and is linked by rail to the port of Lome, the country's capital.

PEPONI (peh-POH-nee)   The Kiswahili word for "paradise, heaven." The Peponi Hotel is a swank tourist hotel on Lamu Island, Kenya.

PERINET (pair-i-NAY)   A town in the eastern rain forests of Madagascar. Perinet is near the Analamaotra-Perinet Reserve, which is considered to be a naturalist's wonder. The majority of the population of Perinet are Bezanozano people whose name is said to mean "small branches." (Could be shortened to **PERI**.)

PETE (PAY-tay)   Kiswahili word meaning "a ring." Although pronounced differently (PEET), it is also a modern English male name derived from Greek meaning "stone."

PHARAOH (FAIR-oh)   The title used for kings of ancient Egypt.

PIANKHI (pee-AHN-kee)   Ruler of Egypt from 747–716 B.C. under the XXV dynasty. Egypt was conquered and ruled for one hundred years by the Nubians (black Africans from eastern Sudan) under the XXV dynasty.

PILI (PEE-lee)   Swahili name used for children who are second born. Kiswahili word meaning "two" or "the second."

PILIPILI (PEE-lee-PEE-lee)   Kiswahili word for "pepper." Coastal Swahili cooking includes "pilipili" dishes, such as prawns Pilipili, which are seasoned with red chili peppers. Pilipili dishes are found in other parts of Africa as well.

POPO (POH-poh)   a) Also called **EWE** (AY-way), this language is spoken by about three million people in Togo, eastern Ghana, and Benin. Popo has its own body of literature. b) A Kiswahili word meaning "bat" (the animal). c) A word commonly used in East Africa for papaya fruit.

PRA (prah)   An Akan of Ghana male name referring to the Pra River.

PUPA (POO-pah)   A Kiswahili word meaning "overeagerness."

R

Song of the Bridesmaids

Oh beautiful bride, don't cry,
Your marriage will be happy.
Console yourself, your husband will be good.
And like your mother and your aunt,
You will have many children in your life;
Two children, three children, four...

Resign yourself, do like all others.
A man is not a leopard,
A husband is not a thunder-stroke,
Your mother was your father's wife;
It will not kill you to work.

It will not kill you to grind the grain,
Nor will it kill you to wash the pots.
Nobody dies from gathering firewood
Nor from washing clothes.

We did not do it to you,
We did not want to see you go,
We love you too much for that.
It's your beauty that did it,
Because you are so gorgeous...
Ah, we see you laugh beneath your tears!

Goodbye, your husband is here
And already you don't seem
To need our consolations...

—Rwandese traditional song

Female

RABENA (rah-BEHN-ah)   A religious festival in honor of the dead of the Afar peoples of the horn of Africa.

RADHIYA (rahd-HEE-yah)   Swahili female name meaning "agreeable."

RAHA (RAH-hah)   A Kiswahili word meaning "happiness, rest."

RAMATULAI (rah-mah-too-LIGH)   A popular female name among the Wolof people of Senegal.

RAMLA (RAHM-lah)   A Swahili female name meaning "fortune teller" or "prophet." Probably derived from the Kiswahili word "ramli" that means "divination."

RANAVALONA (rah-nah-vah-LOO-nah)   Successor to her late husband King Andrianampoinaimerina, Ranavalona was queen of the Merina kingdom of central Madagascar from 1828 until her death in 1861. Later there were two more Merina queens named Ranavalona. Ranavalona III, rumored to be quite beautiful, was the last Merina queen. (Could be shortened to **RANAVA, AVA, AVALONA, AVALON,** or **RANA** (rah-NAH)—itself a Muslim female name meaning "to gaze.")

RANDA (RAHN-dah)   Kiswahili word meaning "to show off, to dance."

RASHAIDA (rah-SHIGH-duh)   Also spelled **RASHIDA,** these are a nomadic, Orthodox Muslim people of the Nubian Desert in northeastern Sudan. The Rashaida are descendents of Bedouins who migrated from Saudi Arabia. Their economy is based on camel trading with Egypt and Arabia. (Could be shortened to **RASHA,** itself a Muslim female name meaning "small gazelle.")

RASHIDA (rah-SHEE-dah)   Also spelled **RASHEEDA, RACHIDA,** and **RAASHIDA.** A Swahili female name meaning "righteous." Also, a Muslim female name meaning "the honest one," or "rightly guided."

RASOHERINA (rah-sohah-HAIR-ee-nah)   Upon the death of her husband King Radama II, she became queen of the

Merina kingdom of central Madagascar serving from 1863 until 1868. Her original name was **RABODO**. Rasoherina means "chrysalis" in the Malagasy language. (Could be shortened to **RASO** or **HERINA**.)

RAZANA (RAH-zahn-ah)   A Malagasy word meaning "ancestors."

RAZIYA (rah-ZEE-yah)   Swahili female name that means "sweet, agreeable."

REGA (RAY-gah)   Also called **BAREGA, VALEGA, LEGA,** and **WAREGA,** these people are based along the Ulindi and Elila rivers in the rain forests of Zaire. They are agriculturalists who speak a Bantu language.

REHANI (ray-HAH-nee)   The Kiswahili word for "a pledge."

REHEMA (reh-HAY-mah, ray-HAY-mah)   A Swahili female name meaning "compassion" and the Kiswahili word for "mercy, grace."

RHAXMA (RAH-mah)   A Somali female name meaning "sweet."

RHAPTA (RAP-tuh)   An ancient, lost city on the east coast of Africa written about by early explorers and traders.

RHODA (ROH-duh)   An island in the Nile River at Cairo, Egypt. The name Rhoda is of Greek origin and means "rose."

RIBA (REE-bah)   A Kiswahili word meaning "interest, usury," as in repaying a loan.

RIVONIA (ri-VOH-nee-uh)   The infamous 1964 trial of Nelson Mandela was dubbed the Rivonia Trial after the small town outside of Johannesburg where it was held. In this trial Mandela was sentenced to life in prison for initiating a political party named Umkonto We Sizwe (Spear of the Nation), which called for non-violent resistance to South Africa's system of apartheid.

ROMA (ROH-muh)   A town in Lesotho near Maseru, the country's capital. Roma is a Hebrew name meaning "exalted, high."

ROSEIRES (roh-SAIR-ays)   Also called **ER ROSEIRES**, this town is found in a beautiful, green area along the Blue Nile River in Sudan.

ROSETTA (roh-ZEHT-uh)   A city at the mouth of the Nile River near Alexandria, Egypt. In Arabic the city is called **RASHID**. This is where the famous Rosetta Stone was found in 1799. The stone was the link needed to decipher ancient Egyptian hieroglyphics. The original stone is on display in the British Museum.

RUSHA (ROO-shah)   A people of Tanzania who speak a Bantu language. Also, a Kiswahili word meaning "to throw off."

RWANDA (roo-AHN-duh)   A small, mountainous, land-locked country located just south of the equator in central Africa. Its size is 10,166 square miles (26,330 square kilometers), almost the size of the state of Maryland. Rwanda has the highest population density in Africa. Its inhabitants include both the world's tallest (Watutsi) and the world's smallest (Pygmy) peoples. Also, Rwanda or Rwandese (technically called Kinyarawanda) is a Bantu language spoken by over two million people in Rwanda and Burundi.

RWEEJ (roo-EHDJ)   Also called **LUEJI** (loo-AY-jee), a female chief of the Lunda peoples of central Africa in the sixteenth century. The union of Chief Rweej and a Luba chief is believed to be the beginning of the Lunda royal line, whose rulers were titled MWATA YAMVO.

Male

RADAMA (rah-DAH-mah)   The name of two kings of Madagascar's Merina Kingdom. Radama I, who began his rule in 1810, brought the process of printing to the island nation. Radama II ruled from 1861–1863.

RADHI (RAHD-hee)   A Kiswahili word meaning "goodwill" and a Muslim male name meaning "accepting."

RAFIKI (rah-FEE-kee)   The Kiswahili word and male name for "friend." **RAFIQ** (rah-FEEK) is the Muslim version of this name. (Could be shortened to **RAFI**, itself a Muslim male name meaning "exalted.")

RAHAD (RAH-had) A river in Ethiopia. The Rahad is three hundred miles (480 kilometers) long and flows from the west of Lake Tana into the Sudan where it joins the Blue Nile.

RAIS (RAH-ees) A Kiswahili word meaning "president." It is probably from the same root word as the Arabic female name RAISA, which means "leader."

RAKANJA (rah-KAHN-jah) Male name of the Muarusha people of Tanzania.

RAMI (RAH-mee) A Muslim male name that is popular in the Sudan and means "love." It is also popular among Christian Arabs of the Middle East.

RAS (rahs) An Ethiopian honorary title equivalent to duke or nobleman. Ras literally means "head."

RAS DASHAN (rahs duh-SHAHN) At 15,158 feet (4,623 meters), this is the highest mountain peak in Ethiopia. It is found in the Simyen mountain range in the north of the country. (Could be shortened to **RAS**, **DASHAN**, or **SHAN**.)

RASHIDI (rah-SHEE-dee) Swahili male name meaning "good council." It is a variation of the Arabic male name **RASHID** (rah-SHEED), which means "rightly guided." Rashidi Mfaume Kawawe became the second vice president of independent Tanzania in 1972.

RESHE (RAY-shay) A people living on the Niger River in northern Nigeria. Also, a Hausa word meaning "branch."

RETTA (RUH-tah) Amharic of Ethiopia male name meaning "he has triumphed, he has won."

REY MALABO (ray mah-LAH-boh) Formerly called Santa Isabel, Rey Malabo is the capital and main market town for cocoa in Equatorial Guinea. It is located on Bioko Island in the Gulf of Guinea. (Could be shortened to **REY**.)

ROBLE Somali male name meaning "born during the rainy season."

ROHO (ROH-hoh) A Kiswahili word for "spirit, soul."

RON (rohn) Also called **BARON** (bah-ROHN) and **CHALA** (CHAH-lah), the Ron are a people of Nigeria. Pronounced "ron" it is a male name derived from Hebrew meaning "joy" or "song."

RONO (ROH-noh)   Henry Rono, a Kenyan, set two world track and field records in 1978: one in Seattle, Washington, for the 3,000-meter steeplechase with a time of 8:05.4, and another in Oslo, Norway, for the 3,000-meter run with a time of 7:32.1.

ROSHANI (roh-SHAH-nee)   The Kiswahili word meaning "balcony."

RUBANI (roo-BAH-nee)   Kiswahili noun meaning "pilot."

RUDI (ROO-dee)   The Kiswahili word meaning "to return."

RUDO (ROO-doh)   A Shona of Zimbabwe name meaning "love."

RUFIJI (roo-FEE-jee)   A river in Tanzania south of Dar-Es-Salaam. (Could be shortened to **FIJI**.)

RUHINDA (roo-HIN-dah)   King Ruhinda ruled the Karagwe and Nkore kingdoms of East Africa (present-day Tanzania and Uganda respectively) in the 1400s.

RYANG'OMBE (ree-ahn-GOHM-bay)   According to the Batutsi people of Rwanda and Burundi, Ryang'ombe, the Ox-Eater, is the god of afterlife and initiation. He is believed to live in the Muhavura volcano in the Virunga Mountains, Rwanda. (Could be shortened to **RYAN**.)

S

Fortitude

Like a she-camel with a large bell
Come from the plateau and upper Haud,
My heat is great.

Birds perched together on the same tree
Call each their own cries,
Every country has its own ways,
Indeed people do not understand each other's talk.

One of my she-camels falls on the road
And I protect its meat,
At night I cannot sleep,
And in the daytime I can find no shade.

I have broken my nose on a stick,
I have broken my right hip,
I have something in my eye,
And yet I go on.
—Anonymous poem written in the Somali language

Female

SAADA (sah-AHD-ah)   Swahili female name meaning "help"
related to the Kiswahili verb "saidia" with the same meaning.
SABA (SAH-bah)   The Kiswahili word for "seven." Pronounced sah-BAH, it is a Muslim female name that is popular
in North Africa and means "morning."

SABI (SAH-bee) A four-hundred-mile-long (644 kilometers) river flowing through eastern Zimbabwe and southern Mozambique into the Indian Ocean. Also, a Muslim female name meaning "little girl."

SABRATHA (SAB-ruh-thuh) Also spelled **SABRATA** (SAB-ruh-tuh) and **SABRANTHA**. A town located west of Tripoli in northern Libya. It is the site of ancient ruins of a Punic-Roman and Byzantine town (46 B.C. to A.D. 300). (Could be shortened to **SABRA** (SAH-bruh), itself a Hebrew name meaning "thorny cactus" and used for those born in Israel.)

SADIO (SAH-dee-oh) A female name in French-speaking countries of West Africa that means "pure."

SAFARA (sah-FAHR-ah) A Wolof of West Africa word meaning "fire."

SAFI (SAH-fee) A Kiswahili word that means "clean, pure." Pronounced SAF-ee, it is a Moroccan coastal resort town where there is an old Portuguese fort and castle.

SAFIA (sah-FEE-yah) Also spelled **SAFIYA, SAFIYEH,** and **SAFIYYAH,** a Swahili and Arabic name meaning "pure, wise" or "lion's share." Safia is a version of the biblical Sophia. Safia was the daughter of a Shaiqiya chief of the Nile area of the Sudan in the 1800s. She was captured while leading soldiers to battle and released unharmed by an invading Turk named Ismail.

SAHAFATRA (sah-hah-FAH-trah) A people of southeast Madagascar whose name means "people of the clearing."

SAHARA (suh-HAHR-uh, suh-HAIR-uh) a) The world's largest desert. The Sahara is approximately 1,000 miles wide (1,600 kilometers) and 3,000 miles long (4,800 kilometers), covering 3,250,000 square miles (8,320,000 square kilometers) of Africa—making it about the size of the United States. Mostly immense tracks of sand and bare rock, it stretches from the Atlantic Ocean in the west to the Nile Valley in the east. Ancient traders of cloth, gold, salt, and slaves used to traverse the Sahara on established trade routes. b) In Arabic the word **SAHRA** (SAH-hrah), the origin of the desert's name, means "the desert, emptiness, wilderness." c) Sahara is an Aramaic and Hebrew female name meaning "moon."

SAHATANDRA (sah-hah-TAHN-drah)   The name of a creek in the Analamaotra-Perinet Reserve in eastern Madagascar. The origin of the name for the creek is disputed by locals. Some legends say that it is named after the oldest man of a nearby village; **TANDRA** is the name of a village girl who drowned in the river, and "saha" is the local word for water; a village woman named Madame Tandra was sacrificed to crocodiles in the creek to prevent the crocodiles from multiplying.

SAHEL (SAH-hehl)   The Sahel refers to the land on the southern edge of the Sahara Desert. Sahel means "shore" as derived from Arabic.

SAIDA (sah-EE-dah)   A Swahili female name meaning "helper" derived from the Kiswahili word "saidia' (sigh-DEE-ah), which means "help." Saida is also popular among Muslims in West Africa.

SAKALAVA (sahk-ah-LAH-vah)   A main city as well as a people living in western Madagascar. The Sakalava people's name means "valley people."

SAKIA (SEHK-ee-ah)   The name given to wooden water wheels powered by oxen used for irrigation in the Sudan. Sakias are found along the Nile River. They are called **ESKALAYS** by the Nubians who live along the Nile River in southern Egypt.

SALAMA (sah-LAH-mah)   Swahili and Muslim female name meaning "peace, safety." It is also a Kiswahili word with the same meaning which is often used in greeting.

SALIMA (sah-LEE-mah)   A town in Central Malawi often used as an overnight stop by people taking excursions to Lake Malawi. Also, a Muslim female name meaning "safe."

SALMA (SAHL-mah)   Another spelling of the Swahili and Muslim female name **SALAMA**.

SAMIA (sah-MEE-ah)   A people of southeastern Uganda and western Kenya who speak a Bantu language. Also, Samia is a Muslim female name meaning "noble" or "lofty."

SANA (SAH-nah)   A Kiswahili word meaning "very much," as in "asante sana," which means "thank you very much." Pronounced sah-NAH, it is a Muslim female name meaning "look upon, gaze."

SANDAWANA (san-duh-WAHN-uh)   A valley in Zimbabwe which is a source of valued emeralds.

SANDI   The historic name used by the Sabiri people of West Africa for their priest-chiefs. Also, a short form of the name ALEXANDRIA.

SANTRA (SAN-truh)   The name of a cook of black African origin mentioned in writings of the ancient Greco-Roman period.

SANTOYA (sahn-TOO-yuh)   A region of Libya.

SANURA (sah-NOOR-ah)   Swahili female name meaning "kitten-like."

SAQQARA (suh-KAHR-uh)   Also spelled **SAKKARA**, the site of the Step Pyramids located outside of Cairo, Egypt. These pyramids, built around 2600 B.C., are the oldest stone structures in the world.

SARA (SAR-uh)   A name used for various groups of people in Chad and Central African Republic who all speak Bongo-Bagirmi. The Sara constitute about 10 percent of the population of the Central African Republic. There are the **SARA GAMBAI, SARA KABA,** and **SARA MBAI** peoples. Also, Sara is a variation of the name **SARAH** that is derived from Hebrew and Arabic meaning "princess, noble." Sarah is a popular name in the Sudan.

SARAFINA (sehr-uh-FEE-nuh)   The title of a Broadway hit musical about life in South Africa's townships. Sarafina comes from Hebrew and means "ardent," referring to the angel with three sets of burning wings that protects God's throne.

SARAKAWA (SAH-rah-KAH-wah)   The name of a town that was founded by a woman. Also the name of a region and a famous hotel in Togo.

SARAN (sah-rahn)   A female name from Guinea and Cote D'Ivoire meaning "joy."

SARAKOLLE (sah-rah-KOH-lay)   Traditionally traders and

sailors, these people are a subgroup of the Mande ethnic group. Their language, also called Sarakolle, or Soninke, is spoken in northern Mali, Burkina Faso, and Mauritania.

SASSANDRA (suh-SAN-druh) A river in Cote D'Ivoire that runs from the western part of the country near the Guinea border into the Atlantic Ocean at a town by the same name. The river is 350 miles (560 kilometers) long.

SATTIMA (suh-TEEM-uh) Also called **LESATIMA** (leh-suh-TEEM-uh), this mountain summit is found in the Aberdares Mountains in Kenya. It is 13,104 feet (3,995 meters) high.

SAUDA (sah-oo-dah) Swahili female name meaning "black-skinned." The Muslim version is pronounced SOOD-ah.

SCYBALE (si-BAHL-ay) According to Roman mythology, Scybale was the helpmate and companion of Simylus. She is depicted as being of African origin.

SEBLE WENGEL (SUHB-luh WEHN-gehl) Amharic and Tigrinya of Ethiopia female name meaning "harvest of the New Testament."

SEKAI (say-KIGH, seh-KIGH) A very popular female name in Zimbabwe. It means "laughter."

SELA a) Ewe of West Africa name for both males and females meaning "savior." b) (SAY-lah) According to Luya of Kenya tradition, Sela was the first woman on earth, equivalent to the biblical Eve. c) Also, a Hebrew female name meaning "rock."

SELAM (SUH-lahm) Female and male name in Amharic and Tigrinya languages of Ethiopia meaning "peace."

SELAMAWIT (suh-lahm-ah-WEET) Amharic and Tigrinya of Ethiopia female name meaning "she is peaceful."

SELIMA (seh-LEE-mah) An oasis town in northern Sudan. Also, a Muslim and Hebrew female name meaning "peace."

SELMA (THEHL-mah) A Muslim female name that is popular in North Africa. It means "secure."

SEMA (SAY-mah) A Kiswahili word meaning "to say or speak." Also, a female name of Greek origin meaning "sprout" or from the Turkish meaning "sky, heavens."

119

SERA (SAY-rah)   The name of a goddess according to Lugisu of Uganda belief.

SHABA (SHAHB-uh)   The southeast province of Zaire, formally called Katanga Province. The capital city of this mineral-rich region is Lubumbashi. Katanga province made an unsuccessful bid for a separate independence soon after Zaire itself had gained independence in 1960. Shaba means "copper" in some Bantu languages, such as Kiswahili. Also, Shaba was a king of Nupe, a Hausa kingdom in Nigeria from 1591–1600.

SHAKI (SHAH-kee)   A city in Western State, Nigeria.

SHANI (SHAH-nee)   Swahili female name meaning "marvellous." Also, the Kiswahili word "shani" translates as "an adventure, something unusual."

SHANTA (SHAHN-tah)   The Kiswahili word for "knapsack."

SHARI (SHAHR-ee)   Also spelled **CHARI**, but pronounced the same. a) The Shari River runs along the northern side of the Ubangi-Shari plateau in central Africa, passing through the Central African Republic and southern Chad into Lake Chad. The river is about 1,400 miles (2,253 kilometers) long. b) The Ubangi-Shari plateau is about the size of the state of Texas. c) Ubangi-Shari was the name of the Central African Republic while under French control.

SHARIFU (shah-REE-foo)   A Kiswahili word that means "noble, honorable." It comes from the same root as the Muslim female name **SHARIFA** (shah-REE-fah) that means "noble."

SHARUFA (shah-ROO-fah)   Swahili and Somali female name meaning "distinguished" and "outstanding."

SHASHI (SHAH-shee)   A river in northeastern Botswana in a densely populated region, mainly inhabited by Tswana-speaking peoples. This river runs 225 miles (362 kilometers) before connecting with the Limpopo River to the south.

SHEBA (SHEE-buh)   The Queen of Sheba's real name was **MAKEDA**, and she was also known as **BELKIS**. According to biblical accounts, the Queen of Sheba ruled over Abyssinia (now Ethiopia). Although written evidence of a liaison is lacking, legend tells of Queen Sheba's dalliance with the Jewish king Solomon, which resulted in their son Menelik I, who later became emperor of Abyssinia. Sheba purportedly brought the House of David and the Ark of the Covenant (through her son Menelik) from Israel to Abyssinia.

SHEBELLE (shuh-BEHL-ee) Also called **WEBBI SHEBELI** (WAY-bee). The Shebelle River runs 1,250 miles (2,000 kilometers) from the highlands in central Ethiopia, down to the southern Somalian Plains, and into swamps near the Indian Ocean. The Shebelle River basin is a fertile area used for cultivation of crops such as bananas and corn.

SHELLA (SHEHL-uh) A resort town on Lamu Island off the east coast of Kenya.

SHENAKDAKHETE (shehn-ahk-dahk-HAY-tay) The first known Candace, or Queen Mother, of the Kingdom of Kush (present-day northern Sudan). She ruled from 170–160 B.C. (Could be shortened to **SHENA**.)

SHENDI (SHEHN-dee) Also spelled **SHENDY** and **SHANDI** (SHAHN-dee), this market town is in northern Sudan on the Nile River. It is near the site of Meroë, the ancient capital of the kingdom of Kush.

SHENI (SHEH-nee) A people of the Zaria region in Nigeria.

SHILA (SHEE-lah) These people live near Lake Mweru in Zambia and in Shaba Province, Zaire. They speak Tabwa, a Bantu language.

SHINASHA Also called **BWORO**, these people of Ethiopia speak a Cushitic language. (Could be shortened to **SHINA** (SHEE-nah), itself a Japanese name meaning "goods [things]" or "virtue.")

SHONA (SHOH-nah) A Bantu language spoken by over four million people in southern Africa which has many dialects and its own body of literature. The Shona, or **MASHONA**, people make up over three-quarters of the population of Zimbabwe. Also, in Kiswahili the word "shona" means "to sew."

121

SIA JATTA (SEE-ah jah-TAH)   According to a Soninke of West Africa folktale, Sia Jatta was a beautiful maiden who was supposed to be sacrificed to a snake called Bida. The saying goes "she's as pretty as Sia Jatta."

SIDYA (SEED-yah)   Also known as **SIDYANKA**, these are a people of Guinea and Guinea-Bissau who speak a language related to Malinke.

SIERRA LEONE (see-AIR-uh lee-OHN)   A hot, humid West African country with a land area of 27,699 square miles (44,567 square kilometers), making it about the size of the state of South Carolina. It has a 210-mile (338 kilometers) coastline on the Atlantic Ocean. Freetown, the capital of Sierra Leone, was founded in 1787 as a haven for freed British slaves. Sierra Leone translates as "Lion Mountain," a name bestowed by the country's first European visitor, a Portuguese explorer, who heard growling thunder coming from the mountains. (The names **SIERRA** and **LEONE** could be used separately.)

SIHANAKA (see-HAH-nah-kah)   A people from northern Madagascar living between the towns of Imerina and Tsimihety. Their name means "marsh people."

SISAY (SEE-sigh)   Amharic of Ethiopia female and male name meaning "omen of good things, a blessing."

SISI (SEE-see)   A version of the Fante of Ghana name **KWESI**, which is given to children born on Sunday. Also, a Kiswahili word meaning "we" or "us."

SITI (SEE-tee)   Swahili name meaning "lady."

SITTINA (si-TEE-nuh)   Historic name used for queens of the Shendi region of the Sudan.

SOFALA (soh-FAHL-ah)   a) This name of Arabic origin means "lowland" and was used to describe the east coast of Africa north of Zanzibar. It was known in full as SOFALATU'L DHABAB, or "lowland of gold." b) Both a region and the name of a port city in Mozambique. It was once an important seaport of the Waqlima kingdom. (Could be shortened to **SOFI**, itself a version of the Greek female name Sophia that means "wisdom.")

122

SOMA (SOH-mah)   A Kiswahili word meaning "to read, to go to school." Also, a Hindi name meaning "moon," for children born on Monday under the astrological sign of Cancer.

SOMALIA (soh-MAH-lee-uh, soh-MAHL-yuh)   The name of this country is believed to come from a Cushitic word meaning "black, dark." Virtually the entire population of Somalia, around 6.5 million, are of the same ethnic group—a rarity in Africa, where most countries have at least two, and sometimes over one hundred, different ethnic groups within their boundaries. The Somali are a Cushitic people who speak a language also called Somali. The majority of Somalis are Muslim and lead a nomadic or semi-nomadic life with livestock raising as their main economic activity. (Could be shortened to **LIA**, itself a Greek and Italian name meaning "bearer of good news," or **SOMA**.)

SOMANYA (soh-MAHN-yah)   A Ga town in the coastal region of Ghana.

SRODA (SROH-duh)   Ghanaian female name meaning "respect."

STAREHE (stah-RAY-hay)   A Kiswahili word meaning "be at peace, at ease." Starahe Academy is a prominent boy's school in Nairobi, Kenya that caters to underprivileged youth. (Could be shortened to **STAR** or **RE**.)

SU (soo)   Also known as the **ISUWU** (ee-SOO-woo), **BIMBIA, ISUBU**, and **SUBU**, these people of Nigeria have a population under five hundred and speak a Bantu language.

SUDIE (soo-dee)   A people of western Niger who speak a Hausa language.

SUSA (soo-sah)   a) A people of Guinea and Sierra Leone who speak the **SUSU** language. In Guinea they are centered around Conakry, the coastal capital. b) The name given to a family (or group) of gorillas found in the Parc National des Volcans, Rwanda.

SADAKA (sah-DAH-kah)   A Swahili male name and a Kiswahili word meaning "a religious offering." Sadaka is the protagonist of a Swahili folktale called "The Three Tests."

SAFI (SAH-fee)   A Muslim male name used in North Africa meaning "exalted."

SALIM (sah-LEEM)   Also **SALIM** or **SALMAN**. A Swahili male name meaning "peace" and a Muslim male name meaning "healthy, safe, complete." Salim Salim is one of Africa's preeminent statesmen. He served in the Tanzanian diplomatic corps in the 1960s and in 1981 was Africa's contender for the post of United Nations Secretary General.

SALONGO (sah-LOHN-goh)   According to Baganda of Uganda custom, the father of twins gives himself this new name.

SAMBURU (sam-BOO-roo)   A nomadic people of northern Kenya who speak a dialect of the Masai language. The Samburu National Park near the northern town of Isiolo, Kenya, is home to rare species of animals, such as the Grevy's zebra, reticulated giraffe, and Somali ostrich. (Could be shortened to **SAM**, itself a short form of the name Samuel, of Hebrew origin and meaning "god hears.")

SAMORI (sah-MOR-ee)   Samori Toure, also known as Samori ibn Lafiya, was a Mandinke emperor who fought off French colonialists in the late nineteenth century.

SARSA DENGEL (SAHR-suh-DUHN-guhl)   Ethiopian male name that literally means "penetration by osmosis." Sarsa Dengel was a Christian emperor of the kingdom of Abyssinia (now Ethiopia) from 1563–1597.

SEF (sehf)   Egyptian male name that means "yesterday" and refers to a lion god.

SEFU (SEH-foo)   A Swahili male name meaning "sword," probably derived from the Arabic word "seif," which also means "sword."

SEKOU (seh-KOO)   A Guinean male name meaning "learned." Sekou Toure, born in 1922, was a trade unionist and politician. He served as first head of state of independent Guinea from 1958–1984. He received the Lenin Peace Prize in 1960.

SELASSIE (suh-LAH-say, seh-LAHS-ee, suh-LAS-ee) Amharic and Tigrinya of Ethiopia male and female name meaning "trinity." It is usually used as a suffix, as in **HAILE** (HIGH-lay) **SELASSIEE**, meaning "power of the trinity."

SEMAKOKIRO (say-mah-koh-KEER-oh) A powerful kabaka (king) of the Buganda kingdom of Uganda in the 1700's.

SENGHOR (SEHN-gor) A male name from Senegal and the Gambia meaning "descendent of the gods." Leopold Sedar Senghor was born in 1906 in Senegal. He was a teacher, poet, and politician who became president of Senegal in 1960. Senghor promoted the concept of "negritude" (translated from French as "blackness") in Africa, which aimed to emphasize traditional African ways as opposed to wholesale adoption of European ways.

SEVERIAN (seh-VAIR-ee-ehn) Of Armenian heritage, Severian was a senator of Sebaste in North Africa. He is a Catholic saint whose feast day is September 9.

SEVERUS (suh-VEER-uhs) Lucius Septimus Severus (A.D. 193–211) was a Roman emperor of African origin.

SHABAAN (shuh-BAN, sheh-BAHN) Muslim male name from East Africa that means "coward." Shabaan Roberts (1901–1962) was an acclaimed Tanzanian poet who was called the "Shakespeare of East Africa." He was the most eminent Kiswahili writer of the twentieth century.

SHABAKA (SHAB-ah-kah) Also called **SHABAKO,** this Kushite king defeated all of Egypt in 716 B.C. He ruled Egypt from 716–702 B.C. under the XXV dynasty, an Aethiopian (meaning black African) dynasty. He was the brother of Piankhi, who preceded him as ruler of Egypt. The ancient Greeks called him **SABACON** (SAB-ah-kon).

SHABATAKA (shab-ah-TAH-kah) An Aethiopian (meaning black African) king who ruled Egypt from 700–688 B.C. under the XXV dynasty. He was also king of Nubia (now eastern Sudan). He was the son of King Shabaka.

SHAMBA (SHAHM-buh)   a) The 93rd ruler of the Bakongo kingdom at Zaire. According to legend, Shamba was a wise and just king who loved to travel. b) A Kiswahili word meaning "farm, plantation."

SHANGO (shahn-GOH)   Also called **KHEVIOSO** (keh-vee-OH-soh) and **IAKOUTA**. According to Yoruba of Nigeria mythology, King Shango Obbato-Kousa is the god of destruction and thunder who is believed to be born in Ife, Nigeria.

SHARIF (shah-REEF)   Also spelled **SHERIF** (sheh-REEF), a Muslim male name meaning "honest" that is popular in Somalia. It is related to **SHARIFU** (shah-REE-foo), a Kiswahili word meaning "noble, honorable."

SHEBITKU (sheh-BIT-koo)   This Aethiopian (meaning black African) king ruled ancient Egypt from 702–690 B.C. under the XXV dynasty. He was also king of Nubia (now eastern Sudan).

SHERBRO (SHUR-broh)   A people of Sierra Leone as well as the name of a river and an island in the country. Sherbro Island, located off the Atlantic coast of Sierra Leone, was the site of the first attempted settlement of black American colonists in 1820.

SHERMARKE (SHUR-mahrk, shur-MAHR-kay)   A Somali male name that means "one who brings good fortune."

SHUBI (SHOO-bee)   A people of Tanzania who live near the northwestern borders with Rwanda and Burundi. They speak a Bantu language.

SIMBA (SIM-buh, SEEM-bah)   A Swahili male name that is popular in eastern Zaire, and a Kiswahili word, both of which mean "lion." Also, a Zezuru of Zimbabwe male name meaning "strength."

SILKO (SIL-koh)   This Nubian king, who was known as a king of the Aethiopians (meaning black Africans), defeated Blemmyes around A.D. 545 Silko converted himself, and thus his kingdom , to Christianity around A.D. 543.

SONNI ALI (SOO-nee-A-lee)   Also spelled **SUNNI ALI**, he was emperor of Songhai, a former West African empire, from

1464–1492. Sonni Ali's military conquests expanded the empire west into Mali and east into Hausaland.

SUDI (soo-dee) A Swahili male name and Kiswahili word meaning "success" or "luck."

SULAIMAN (soo-lay-MAHN) Also spelled **SULEIMAN,** this Muslim male name is popular in North Africa and means "peaceful." It is a variation of the Hebrew name Solomon. Sulaiman Dama was an early ruler of the ancient West African kingdom of Songhai.

SULE (soo-lay) West African male name meaning "adventurous."

SULTAN (sool-TAHN) A Swahili male name meaning "ruler."

SUNDIATA (soon-dee-AH-tah) Also spelled **SUNDYATA, SOUNDIATA,** and **SUNJATA,** this Guinean male name means "hungry lion." King Sundiata, a Malinke chief known as the Lion King, conquered the kingdom of Ghana and founded the empire of Mali in the thirteenth century A.D.

SUNNY (SUHN-nee) King Sunny Ade (ah-DAY) is a Nigerian musician who has been dubbed Master Guitarist and Minister of Enjoyment. His back-up band, called the African Beats, has twenty-three members. Sunny Ade's style of juju music is called synchro system. He was born in 1946 with the name Sunday Adeniyi.

SURI (soor-ee) A town in northern Sudan, as well as a people living in Sudan and the Borne Plateau in Ethiopia who speak a Didinga-Murle language.

T

Every dog has his day.
— Terence, from his play, *The Eunuch*

Female

TABANA (tah-BAH-nah) A Kiswahili word meaning to "make incantations."

TABIA (tah-BEE-ah) A Swahili name meaning "talents," and a Kiswahili word meaning "character, nature."

TABORA (tuh-BOHR-uh) The capital of Tanzania's western region. The city was founded in 1820 by Zanzabari traders, whose trade routes from Lake Victoria to Lake Nyasa and from Lake Tanganyika to the Tanzanian coast met at Tabora. It is estimated that some 500,000 persons involved in trade used to pass through Tabora every year.

TAFUI (tah-FWEE) A Mina of Togo female name meaning "to appreciate God; Glory to God."

TAITA (tah-EE-tah) The Taita-Taveta Hills jut up from Kenya's flat, arid southern region. A group of Bantu peoples called the Taita live in this area.

TAITU (TAH-EE-too, TIGH-too) Taitu, wife of Menelik II, was empress of Ethiopia at the turn of the twentieth century.

TAJA (TAH-jah) Kiswahili word meaning "to mention, to name."

TALINGA (tah-LEEN-gah) These people live in the Ruwenzori Mountains in Uganda and Zaire, and speak a Bantu language. (Could be shortened to **TAL** [tahl], itself a Hebrew female name meaning "jewel" or "dew.")

128

TAMARIN A town and bay on the western side of the island country of Mauritius.

TAMATAVE (TAHM-mah-TAHV, tam-uh-TAHV) Also called **TOAMASINA** (toh-uh-muh-SEE-nuh). A large coastal city in northeast Madagascar, it is the country's main harbor. (Could be shortened to **TAMA**, itself a Native American name meaning "jewel.")

TANA (TAH-nuh) a) Also known as Lake **TSANA, TZANA** (TSAH-nuh), and **DEMBEA**. Lake Tana in Ethiopia's northern highlands is the source of the Blue Nile. This crater lake measures 1,400 square miles (3,626 square kilometers), making it the largest lake in Ethiopia. It sits about 5,774 feet high. b) The Tana River in Kenya flows 750 miles (1,200 kilometers) from the town of Meru at the foot of Mount Kenya into the Indian Ocean. c) Another Tana River is found in southern Ghana.

TANA GALANA (TAH-nah-gah-LAH-nah) A people of eastern Kenya who are culturally reminiscent of Somalis. They are Muslim and lead a nomadic lifestyle.

TANALA (tah-NAH-lah) A people of eastern Madagascar. The Tanala engage in woodcutting and rice cultivation. Their name means "people of the forest."

TANDRA (TAHN-drah) Female name from Madagascar meaning "mole" or "beauty marks," inferring that the girl is beautiful.

TANGA (TANG-guh) a) Tanzania's second largest city and a seaport. It is the historic center of Swahili literature. Tanga city is located in Tanga province in the country's northeast. b) The Tanga people, also called **BATANGA**, live in Cameroon and speak a Bantu language. c) Tanga (TAHN-gah) is the Kiswahili word for "sail."

TANISHA (tah-NEE-shah) Hausa of West Africa name for females born on Monday. (Could be shortened to **TANI** (TAH-nee), itself a Japanese female name meaning "valley.")

TARAJA (tah-RAH-jah) The Kiswahili word for "hope." (Could be shortened to **TARA** or **RAJA**.)

TARANA (tahr-AH-nah) A Hausa of Nigeria name for females born during the day.

129

TASSILI (tah-SEE-lee) Tassili n' Ajjer (NAH-jur) is an immense sandstone plateau in the Sahara Desert in southeastern Algeria where Stone Age rock paintings show that the Sahara was once green and abundant. Tassili n' Ajjer has been dubbed "the largest open-air museum in the world."

TATA (TAH-tah) a) The Kikuyu of Kenya word for "aunt." b) A town in southern Morocco. c) A Kiswahili word meaning "to tangle, to perplex."

TATU (TAH-too) Swahili name for third–born children, and the Kiswahili word for "three."

TAVAVICH (tah-vah-VICH) A chief's daughter, Tavavich became the first wife of Emperor Theodore II of Abyssinia (now Ethiopia) in the nineteenth century.

TAVETA (tah-VEH-tuh) A people living in the Taita-Taveta Hills of southeast Kenya. They speak a Bantu language.

TAWANYA (tah-WAHN-yah) A Kiswahili word meaning "to scatter."

TAWIA (TAH-yoo-ah, TAH-wee-ah) Ga of Ghana unisex name for the first child born after twins.

TEMA (TAY-muh) A principal city of southeastern Ghana located on the Gulf of Guinea. Also, an Egyptian word for "city."

TERA (TAY-rah) a) A people of Bornu and Bauchi regions of Nigeria who speak a Chadic language. b) A town in western Niger. c) A form of the name Theresa, which comes from Greek and means "reaper."

TERU (TUH-roo) Amharic of Ethiopia female name meaning "good." It is most often used in combination with other names, as in **TERUWORQ** (TUH-roo-WURK), which means "good gold."

TESO (TEH-soh) An ethnic group of Uganda making up about 8 percent of the country's population. They are Nilotic people who lead a nomadic lifestyle.

TISSISSAT (TIS-uh-saht) Also called **TESSISAT** (tehs-uh-SAHT) and the Blue Nile Falls. The Tississat Falls are located on the Blue Nile River not far from Lake Tana in Ethiopia. They are one-hundred-forty-feet (42.7 meters) high.

Tississat is an Amharic word meaning "smoke of fire." (Could be shortened to **TISSI** or **TESSI**.)

THABANA NTLENYANA (tah-BAHN-uh nt-lehn-YAHN-uh) At 11,425 feet (3,482 meters), this is the highest peak in southern Africa. The name means "little black mountain" in the local language.

TIMA (TEEM-ah) A people living in the Nuba Hills of Sudan who speak a Katle language. Also, Tima is a short form of the Greek name Timandra, which means "honor."

TINI (TEE-nee) A people of Zaire who speak a Bantu language.

TISA (TEE-sah) Swahili name for ninth-born children. Also, the Kiswahili word for the number nine.

TITI (tee-TEE) Nigerian female name meaning "flower."

TITISHANA (tee-tee-SHAHN-ah) This young girl is the protagonist of an African legend called "The Sacred Cat."

TIYE (TEE-ay) The wife of Amenhotep III and queen of Egypt from 1415–1340 B.C. This commoner queen of Nubian (meaning black African) origin gave birth to Tutankamen when she was fifty years old.

TOTIT (TOH-tit) An Amharic of Ethiopia word for a female monkey. It is used in Ethiopia as a nickname for girls.

TSWANA (TSWAH-nuh) A Bantu people numbering over three million who live in Botswana and South Africa. They speak Setswana. Botswana means "the land of the Tswana."

TULA (TOO-lah) These people live in the Bauchi region of Nigeria. Also, Tula is a Hindi name for children born under the astrological sign of Libra.

TULI (TOO-lee) A safari park in southern Zimbabwe. b) A Kiswahili noun meaning "quiet, tranquil."

TULIA (too-LEE-ah) A Kiswahili verb meaning "to be calm, to be tranquil." Spelled **TULLIA**, it is a female name derived from Latin meaning "third."

TULLA TULLA (TOO-luh TOO-luh) A phrase from the Lingala language of Zaire that means "couldn't care less."

TUSIA (TOO-see-uh) A people living in Cote D'Ivoire.

TUTI (TOO-tee)   Tuti Island sits in the middle of the Nile River at Khartoum, the capital of the Sudan.

TUTSI (TOOT-see)   This royal dynasty ruled kingdoms in what is now Rwanda and Burundi up to the 1960s. People of the Tutsi line are called Watutsi.

Male

TABAN (toh-BAHN)   Somali and Ugandan male name. Taban Lo Liyong is a Ugandan literary critic and poet. His works include *Fixions, Eating Chiefs,* and *Frantz Fannon's Uneven Ribs.*

TABU (TAH-boo)   Tabu Ley Rochereau is a world-famous Zairois jazz musician. His genre of music is called "soukous," which means "having a good time."

TAFI (TAH-fee)   A people of Togo with a population under one thousand.

TAHARKA (tah-HAHR-kah)   Also spelled **TAHARQA**, this Aethiopian (meaning black African) king ruled Egypt from 690–664 B.C. under the XXV dynasty. Taharka was the nephew of King Shabaka. He is referred to as **TIRHAKAH** (tir-HAY-kah) in the Bible's Old Testament.

TALODI (teh-LOH-dee)   A people of Sudan with a very small population. They speak a Koalib-Tagoi language. Talodi is also a town in the Nuba Mountains of west central Sudan. (Could be shortened to **TAL**, itself a Hebrew name meaning "dew, rain.")

TAMIRAT (TAM-i-rot)   Amharic of Ethiopia male name meaning "miracle."

TANO (TAH-noh)   a) Ghanaian male name after the Tano River. b) In Togo mythology, Tano was a river god. c) The Kiswahili word for the number five.

TANGIER (tan-JEER)   Also spelled **TANGIERS** (tan-JEERZ), a port city on the Straits of Gibraltar in northern Morocco.

TARIKU (tah-REE-koo)   Amharic of Ethiopia male name meaning "the story behind, the events surrounding his birth."

TASHFIN (tahsh-FEEN) Yussef ibn Tashfin was an Almoravid soldier and monk who conquered Morocco, Western Algeria, and much of Spain in the eleventh century A.D. He founded the Moroccan city of Marrakesh in A.D. 1062.

TAU (TAH-OO) A Tswana of Botswana male name meaning "lion."

TAYE (TAH-yay) Amharic of Ethiopia male name that means "he has been seen."

TEFERI (tuh-FUH-ree) Amharic and Tigrinya of Ethiopia male name meaning "one who is ferocious, one who is feared (by his rivals)."

TEGENE (tuh-guh-NAY) Amharic of Ethiopia male name meaning "my protector."

TEKA (TUH-kah) Amharic of Ethiopia male name meaning "he has replaced." For example, meaning he has replaced his father as head of the family.

TEKLE (TUHK-lay) Amharic and Tigrinya of Ethiopia male name which literally means "my plant" and implies "I gave my seed to him." Tekle Afewerk is an Ethiopian artist who works with murals, stained glass, mosaic, sculpture, and frescoes. He was born in Ankobar, Shoa Province, Ethiopia, in 1932, and studied in London.

TEM a) The Temba people of northern Togo speak this language, which belongs to the Gur language family. b) (tehm) The oldest god and the one responsible for creating the world, according to ancient Egyptian texts, called collectively *Books of the Dead*. c) An XI dynasty queen of Egypt. d) Pronounced "taym," an English Gypsy name meaning "country."

TERENCE (TEHR-uhns) A popular comic-poet of ancient Rome who wrote *The Eunuch* and other plays. This dark-skinned man was originally a slave in the Roman city-state of Carthage in North Africa (in present-day Tunisia). His full name was **PUBLIUS TERENTIUS AFER**. The name Terence is of Latin origin and means "smooth, tender."

TERTULLIAN (tuhr-TUL-yuhn, tuhr-TUL-ee-uhn) Tertullian (A.D. 160–230) was a prominent figure in ancient Rome. He was a priest of the Church of Carthage and was of Aethiopian (meaning black African) origin. (Could be shortened to **TULLI**).

TESFAYE (tuhs-FAH-yay, TUHS-figh)   Amharic and Tigrinya of Ethiopia male name meaning "my hope."

TESSEMA (tuh-SUH-mah)   Amharic of Ethiopia male name meaning "he has been heard, people listen to him."

TEWODROS (tay-WOH-drohs)   Ethiopian male name, which is a version of the Greek name Theodore, which means "gift of god." Tewodros II, also known as Theodore II, was king of Abyssinia (now Ethiopia) from 1855-1868. He was born Kedaref Kassa in 1816 in Kwara District. Tewodros was defeated by British troops and opposing Ethiopian forces in 1868 at Magdala, his mountain fortress. Faced with defeat, he killed himself.

THABAZIMBI (tahb-uh-ZIM-bee)   A small town in South Africa in the Transvaal.

TIGG   The blacksmith caste of Wolof people of Senegal and Gambia, traditionally considered a lower societal class.

TOBECHUKWU (toh-bay-CHOO-koo)   Ibo of Nigeria male name meaning "praise God." (Could be shortened to **TOBY**).

TOGO (TOH-goh)   A small West African country on the Atlantic Ocean. It is about two times the size of the state of Maryland. The country's name means "edge of the water" in the Ewe language.

TOMI (TOH-mee)   Kalarbari of Nigeria male name meaning "the people." Also, a Japanese name meaning "rich."

TONYE (TOHN-yay)   Ijaw of Niger male name.

TORIKO (toh-REE-koh)   A people of Zaire who speak Liko, a Bantu language.

TOURE (too-RAY)   A Guinean surname indicating that the family belongs to the Maninka or Soussou ethnic group. Sekou Toure was the first Guinean head of state (see **SEKOU**). Toure Kunda is the name of a Senegalese musical group composed of three brothers.

TRUDO (troo-DOH)   Agaja (ah-GAH-zhah) Trudo was king of Dahomey (now Benin) in the early 1700s.

TSAVO (SAHV-oh, TSAHV-oh)   Tsavo is the largest national park in Kenya. It is divided into two sections, Tsavo West and Tsavo East, at the main Nairobi-Mombasa highway. Tsavo is particularly known for its large population of elephants. There is also a river in southeastern Kenya called Tsavo.

TUMTUM (TOOM-toom)   A people living in the Nuba Hills of Sudan with a population under two thousand.

TUNDE (TOON-day)   A popular Yoruba of Nigeria male name. It is the short form for numerous names ending in **TUNDE**, such as **BABATUNDE**, meaning "father returns," **OLATUNDE**, which means "honor or wealth returns," **OMOTUNDE**, meaning "a child returns," and **AKINTUNDE** for "bravery returns."

TUTU (TOO-too)   a) West African male name meaning "cliff dweller." b) An African surname. Examples: 1. Anglican Archbishop Desmond Tutu is one of the most prominent Christian leaders campaigning against the system of apartheid in South Africa, his homeland. He won the Nobel Peace Prize in 1984. 2. King Osei Tutu of Kumasi ruled the Ashanti kingdom of Ghana during the seventeenth century. Tutu initiated the Ashanti legend of the golden stool, which he claimed fell from the heavens into his lap proving his divine right to the throne.

TYRO (TIGH-roh)   Of African origin, Tyro was Cicero's secretary who is credited with inventing shorthand in 63 B.C. Cicero was a famous Roman philosopher and statesman.

U, V, *and* W

The frog says, "Although I have nothing, I always have my hop."

-Vai of West Africa proverb

Female

UBORO (oo-BOHR-ah)   The Kiswahili word meaning "excellence."

UCHENNA (oo-CHEEN-ah)   Ibo of Nigeria female name meaning "God's will."

UHURU (oo-HOO-roo)   Kiswihili word meaning "freedom."

ULU (oo-LOO)   Ibo of Nigeria name for second-born females.

UMM (oom)   Muslim female name popular in North Africa. It means "mother" and refers to the Prophet Muhammed's daughter Umm Kulthum.

URENNA (oo-REEN-ah)   Ibo of Nigeria female name meaning "father's pride."

VAI (vigh)   A people of southwest Liberia and Sierra Leone and their language which belongs to the Mande language group. The Vai have their own alphabet which was created in the 1830's, making it one of the first local languages in West Africa to be adapted into written script.

VALIHA (vah-LEE-hah)   A Malagasy harp (instrument).

VANA (VAH-nah)   A Kongo word meaning "To grant."

VASHA (VAH-shah)   A language spoken in South Africa,

VENDA (VEHN-duh)   a) A Bantu people of South Africa and Zimbabwe and their language. b) The name of one of South

Africa's so-called homeland states. c) A Mende of West Africa word meaning "to be full." d) A Kongo word for "to miss."

VERENA (vair-EHN-uh)   A Catholic saint who, according to legend, was born in the third century in Thebaid, Egypt. She moved to Switzerland where she served the poor. Her feast day is September 1. Verena is a female name of Latin origin meaning "one who venerates the Lord" or "sacred wisdom."

VICTORIA (vik-TOHR-ee-uh)   a) Also known as **VICTORIA NYANZA** (nee-AHN-zuh, nigh-AHN-zuh), Lake Victoria is bordered by Kenya, Uganda, and Tanzania in east Africa. Measuring 26,828 square miles (69,452 square kilometers), it is the second largest freshwater lake in the world, and the third largest lake, after the Caspian Sea and Lake Superior. It is primarily filled by rainwater drain-off from nearby tropical forests and is the source of the White Nile. The lake is not a recreational lake, as it is inhabited by crocodiles, and hippopotami, and is infested with bilharzia organisms. b) Victoria Falls are found on the Zambezi River between Zambia and Zimbabwe. The falls are 4,500 feet (1,372 meters) wide and plunge 355 feet (108 meters). c) Victoria is the capital of the East African island country of Seychelles. d) Victoria is a female name derived from Latin meaning "victorious."

VITA (VEET-ah)   a) A people found in the Central African Republic and also in the Wau Mboro region of the Sudan, where they are called **GOLO**. They speak a Banda-Gbaya-Ngbandi language. b) A Zairois football (soccer) team that is one of Africa's leading clubs. c) A Kiswahili word for "war, battle." d) A Luya of Kenya male name meaning "war." d) An Italian word and female name that means "life."

WAGAYE (wah-GAH-yay)   Amharic of Ethiopia female name meaning "my sense of value" or literally "my price."

WALASMA (wah-LAHS-mah)   The name of the royal family who ruled the Awfat Sultanate (a Muslim state) in eastern Ethiopia and northern Somalia from the thirteenth through the sixteenth centuries.

WALDA (WAHL-dah) A village in northern Kenya not far from the Ethiopian border. Also, a European female name meaning "forest" or "rule."

WAMBUI (wahm-BOO-ee) or **WAMBOI** (wahm-BOH-ee) A popular name for females of the Kikuyu peoples of Kenya. It means "singer" and refers to one of the nine daughters of Gikuyu and Mumbi, the legendary founders of the Kikuyu tribe.

WANDA (WAHN-dah) a) A people living in Tanzania south of Lake Rukwa who speak a Bantu language. b) A kiswahili word meaning "get fat." c) (wahn-DAH) A Hausa of West Africa word for "who." d) (WAHN-duh) A female name derived from Teutonic meaning "wanderer."

WANGARI (wahn-GAHR-ee) A popular Kikuyu of Kenya female name. Wangari Maathai (mah-THIGH) was the first woman in Kenya to earn a Ph.D. and the first female to teach at the University of Nairobi. She now heads an environmental organization called The Greenbelt Movement.

WANJIRU (wahn-JEER-oo) or **WANJIRO** (wahn-JIR-oh) A common name among females of the Kikuyu people of Kenya. Wanjiru refers to one of the nine daughters of Gikuyu and Mumbi, the legendary founders of the Kikuyu tribe.

WANKIE (WAHNG-kee) The former name for a town on the Zambezi River in southwestern Zimbabwe. Now called **HWANGE** (HWAHNG-gee), this town is located near the largest coal mine in Africa, and is one of Zimbabwe's major game parks, the Wankie Game Reserve.

WANYIKA (wah-NYEE-kah) A Swahili name meaning "of the bush."

WUB (wuhb) Amharic of Ethiopia female name meaning "gorgeous, beautiful."

Male

UBANI (oo-BAH-nee) A Kiswahili noun meaning "incense."

UCHECHI (oo-chay-CHEE) Ibo of Nigeria male name meaning "God's will."

UCHI (OO-chee)   A Kiswahili word for "nakedness." Also, a short form of the male name **UCHECHI** (see above).

UJIJI (OO-JEE-jee)   The town in Tanzania near Lake Tanganyika where Henry Morton Stanley, reporter for the *New York Herald,* located the Scottish missionary and explorer Dr. David Livingstone in 1871. Thus the famous quote, "Dr. Livingstone, I presume?"

USUTU (oo-SOO-too)   A Basotho of Lesotho word meaning "brown," used to name the Usutu River in Swaziland.

UTHMAN (OOT-MAHN)   A Muslim male name popular in North Africa. It means "friend of the Prophet." Shehu Uthman dan Fodio (1754–1817) was a Fulani leader who held a successful jihad, or holy war, resulting in the creation of the Fulani-Hausa Empire of Sokoto (now northern Nigeria). He was also author of classic Islamic texts.

VALERIAN (vuh-LEER-ee-uhn)   A Catholic saint (A.D. 377–457) who was Bishop of Abenza, Africa during the rule of the Vandals. Valerian is a Latin male name meaning "to be strong, valiant."

VEZO (VEH-zoh)   Living in the southwestern coast of Madagascar, the Vezo are a clan of the Sakalava ethnic group (see **MIKEA**). The Vezo clan primarily make a living from the sea, thus their name, which means "people of the paddle."

VINZA (VEEN-zah)   A people of Tanzania with a small population who speak a Bantu language.

VUKANI (voo-KAHN-ee)   The word meaning "wake up" in Xhosa, a language of South Africa. Vukani is the title of a song written by Hugh Masekela and sung by Miriam Makeba.

WACHIRU (wah-CHEER-oo)   Kikuyu of Kenya male name meaning "lawmaker's son."

WALEED (wah-LEED)   Also spelled **WALID**, this Muslim male name is popular in North Africa. It means "newborn."

WALI (WAH-lee)   An Appa of West Africa word for "moon." b) A Kiswahili word meaning "cooked rice." c) A Muslim male name meaning "governs all."

WAMBUA (wahm-BOO-ah)   A Kamba of Kenya male name meaning "born during rainy season."

WAMOCHA (wah-MOH-chah)   A Luhya of Kenya name meaning "never satisfied."

WANG'OMBE (wah-NGOHM-bay)   A Kikuyu of Kenya male name for "one who owns many cows." Derived from "ng'ombe," the Kiswahili word for "cattle."

WANJALA (wahn-JAH-lah)   A Luya of Kenya male name meaning "famine." Probably related to the Kiswahili words for famine "njaa kuu," which translate literally as "great hunger."

WANJOHI (wahn-JOH-hee)   Kikuyu of Kenya male name meaning "brewer."

WASIFU (wah-SEE-foo)   A Kiswahili word meaning "to describe." Probably from the same root as **WASSIF** (wah-SEEF), a Muslim male name meaning "the describer."

WEKESA (way-KAY-sah)   A Luhya of Kenya name meaning "born during harvest time."

WERE (WAY-ray)   Meaning "father of grace," this name is used by the Kikuyu of Kenya for their god of creation.

WOLE (WOH-lay)   Nigerian Wole Soyinka is a university lecturer, novelist, and playwright. Soyinka won the Nobel Prize for Literature in 1986. He runs his own theater company called "Masks." He was born in 1934 in Abeokuta, Nigeria. Soyinka's plays include *Madmen and Specialists* (1971), *Kongi's Harvest* (1965), *The Strong Breed* (1962), and *Dance of the Forests* (1960). His novels include *The Interpreters.*

X and Y

What a Day!

What a day, when the morning air does not resound
with the pounding of yams!
What a day when I listened in vain to hear them sift
the flour!
When the frying pots do not simmer with the fricassee
of rabbits and birds.
What a day when the expert wakes up under the
shadow of starvation!
— Traditional poem of the Yoruba people of Nigeria

Female

XETSA (heht-SAH)   Ewe of Ghana female name for one of a
pair of female twins.

XHOSA (KOH-sah)   About four million Xhosa people live in
eastern Cape Province and Transkei, South Africa. Traditionally, the Xhosa were cattle herders and farmers. Their language, also called Xhosa, belongs to the Bantu language
family and uses clicking sounds.

XOIS (ZOH-uhs)   Located near the city of Busiris, this was
the ancient capital of the XIV Egyptian dynasty (around
seventeenth century B.C.).

YALA (YAH-lah)   The Yala River in Kenya flows into Lake
Victoria.

YANIKA (yah-NEE-kah)   A Kongo word meaning "to dry in
the sun."

YASMIN (YAHS-min, yahs-MEEN)   Muslim female name that is popular in Somalia. It means "jasmine," symbolizing friendliness and sweetness.

YATIMA (yah-TEE-mah)   This Kiswahili word means "an orphan."

YEHUDIT (yeh-HOO-dit)   A tenth-century Falasha (Ethiopian Jewish) queen rumored to be quite beautiful as well as militaristic. Queen Yehudit conquered and reigned over the kingdom of Axum for forty years. Yehudit is a Hebrew female name meaning "praise," referring to the biblical heroine Judith.

YENDI (YEHN-dee)   A town in northeastern Ghana.

YESHI (YEH-shee)   Amharic of Ethiopia female name meaning "for a thousand." It is often used in combination with other names such as **YESHI EMEBET** (UHM-uh-bit), which means "mistress of a thousand people."

YOLA (YOH-luh)   A city in eastern Nigeria on the Benue River near the Cameroon border. Pronounced YOH-lah, a Hausa word for "firefly."

YORUBA (YOH-roo-bah)   A people of southwest Nigeria, central Togo, and Benin numbering over seventeen million. They speak a Kwa language, also called Yoruba, in which extensive literature is written. Traditionally the Yoruba are farmers. Yoruba means "the meeting place" in reference to Yorubaland, which was formed of peoples from different tribes.

YUBI (YOO-bee)   Also spelled **JUBY**, Cape Yubi is found in southwestern Morocco on the Atlantic coast.

Male

XOLA (KOH-lah)   A Xhosa of South Africa male name meaning "stay in peace."

YACOB (YAH-kohb)   Amharic and Tigrinya male name referring to the biblical Jacob.

YAHYA (YAH-yah)   a) Swahili male name meaning "God's gift." b) Arabic male name for biblical John the Baptist and meaning "living." c) Yahya bin Ibrahim was a eleventh-century Berber chief whose pilgrimage to Mecca led to the placing of a Muslim missionary in his home in the western Sahara. This event is considered the cornerstone of the Almoravid movement. d) Yahya Hakki is a modern Egyptian writer.

YANNICK (YAH-nik)   Yannick Noah, born in Cameroon, now resides in France, where he is a professional tennis player and has a hit reggae song called "Saga Africa."

YAO (YAH-oo)   Ewe of Ghana name for males born on Thursday. The Akan version of this name is **YAWO** (YAH-woh).

YAVU (YAH-voo)   A Lunda of Zaire name. Yavu, a Yirung, and Yavu, a Nawej, were seventeenth-century rulers of the Lunda kingdom.

YEKUNO AMLAK (yah-KOO-noo AHM-lahk)   This male name means "let him be good to God" in Ge'ez, an ancient language of Ethiopia. Yekuno Amalak was an Amharic prince who became emperor of the kingdom of Axum (today northern Ethiopia) in the thirteenth century A.D. He claimed to be a descendent of Solomon and Sheba, thus restoring the Solomonic royal line.

YERA (YEH-rah)   A male name from southern Africa that means "warrior."

YERODIN (yeh-ROO-deen)   A Congolese male name meaning "studious."

YESUTO (YAY-soot-oh)   An Ewe of Ghana male name meaning "belongs to Jesus."

YETA (YAY-tah)   A Lozi of South Africa male name. Yeta I, Yeta II, and Yeta III were rulers of the former Lozi kingdom.

YOHANCE (yoh-HAHN-say)   This Hausa of West Africa male name means "God's gift" and refers to the biblical John the Baptist.

YOHANNES (yoh-HAHN-uhs)   Ethiopian male name referring to the biblical John. Yohannes was a Christian king and emperor of Axum (now northern Ethiopia) from A.D. 1667 to 1682. Yohannes IV was king of Axum from A.D. 1872 to 1887.

He was a former governor of Tigray who was then known as DEJAZMATCH ("general") KASSA MERCHA.

YONAS (YOH-nahs)   Ethiopian male name referring to the biblical Jonah.

YOUSSOU (YOO-soo)   Youssou N'Dour is a Senegalese musician who sings in Wolof, a language of Senegal and The Gambia. Born in Dakar in 1959, Youssou began singing in public at the age of twelve.

YULISA (yoo-LEE-sah)   Yulisa Amadu Maddy is a writer from Sierra Leone. His works include the play *Obasai* and the novel *No Past, No Present, No Future.*

YUSUF (yoo-SOOF, YOO-suf)   Swahili and Muslim male name meaning "the beautiful" or "he shall increase," referring to the biblical Joseph. It is also spelled **YUSSEF** (YOO-sehf) and **YUSEF,** and is a popular name in Somalia.

Z

God bless Africa,
Let her fame spread far and wide!
Hear our prayer:
May God bless us!

Come, Spirit, Come!
Come! Holy Spirit!
Come and bless us, her children!
—Zimbabwe national anthem,
words written collectively

Female

ZAGORA (zah-GOH-rah)   A main town in the Dra Valley of eastern Morocco.

ZAHINA (zah-HEE-nah)   Swahili female name popular in Tanzania.

ZAHRA (ZAH-rah)   Also spelled **ZAHARA** (zah-HAH-rah), a Swahili and Muslim female name meaning "flower."

ZAINABU (zah-ee-NAH-boo)   A Swahili female name meaning "beautiful" and referring to Muhammed's eldest daughter.

ZAJI (ZAH-jee)   This word means "woman" in Tappa language of West Africa.

ZAKIYA (zah-KEE-yah)   Swahili female name meaning "smart, intelligent."

ZALA (ZAH-lah)   A people from southwest Ethiopia who speak a Cushitic language.

ZALIKA (zah-LEE-kah)   Swahili female name meaning "well-born."

ZANZI (ZAHN-zee)   Also **EBEZANZI,** a traditional name used for the upper caste of the Ndebele people of South Africa and Zimbabwe. They are believed to be direct descendents of those families who broke away from the Zulu kingdom in the early nineteenth century, thereby creating the Ndebele peoples.

ZARIA (ZAH-ree-uh)   The capital of North-Central State Nigeria and home to Nigeria's largest university. It was an important ancient Hausa city-state beginning around A.D. 1,000.

ZAUDITU (ZOW-DEE-too)   Also spelled **ZAWDITU,** an Amharic of Ethiopia female name meaning "she is the crown." Zauditu became empress of Ethiopia in 1913, upon the death of her father, Emperor Menelik II. She ruled until her mysterious death in 1930.

ZAWADI (zah-WAH-dee)   Swahili female name and Kiswahili word meaning "a gift, a present."

ZAWILA (zah-WEE-lah)   A town in Fezzan in West Africa located along one of the trans-Sahara roadways.

ZAZZAU (zah-ZOW)   The former name of the region ruled by the Zaria kingdom in what is now northern Nigeria.

ZEILA (ZAY-lah)   Also spelled **ZEILAH** and **SAYLAH,** a Somali port town on the Gulf of Aden. Zeila was capital of the former Muslim state of Ifat and a notable port along ancient Red Sea trade routes.

ZEINAB (ZAY-nab)   Popular Somali female name meaning "good."

ZELA (ZAY-lah)   A people of Shaba Province, Zaire. Also a variation of the Hebrew female name Zoe.

ZELLA (ZEH-lah)   A town in northern Libya.

ZENA (ZAY-nah)   Ethiopian name meaning "news" or "fame." Also, it is a Persian name meaning "woman" and a Hebrew name meaning "stranger."

ZENATA (zay-NAH-tah)   More commonly known as BERBERS, the Zenata are an extensive group of languages

146

and peoples of northern Africa found in Morocco, Algeria, Tunisia, Libya, and Egypt. Traditionally the Zenata inhabited the Atlas Mountain ranges and were semi-nomadic.

ZERMA (ZUR-mah) Also called **JERMA, DJERMA,** and **ZABERMA/SONRAI.** An agriculturalist people of West Africa who constitute about 20 percent of Niger's population, living mainly in the southern part of the country. Zerma is also the name of their language.

ZINSA (ZEEN-sah) A name from Benin for a female twin.

ZIZI (ZEE-zee) a) A Kiswahili word meaning "animal shelter." b) In the 1600s, an Nguni people called the Zizi were the first Bantu speakers to migrate into the area now called Lesotho.

ZOLA (ZOH-lah) Congolese female name meaning "productive," and Xhosa of South Africa male name meaning "quietness."

ZUHURA (zoo-HOO-rah) A Swahili female name.

ZULA (zoo-luh) A port town in Eritrea (the contested former northern province of Ethiopia) on the Gulf of Zula near the city of Massawa.

ZUMA (zoo-mah) The name of the main market in Antananarivo, the capital of Madagascar. It is said to be the world's second largest market.

ZVISHAVANE (zvee-shuh-VAH-nay) Previously called **SHABANI** (shuh-BAHN-ee), this is a town in central Zimbabwe.

ZWENA (ZWAY-nah) or **ZUWENA** (zoo-WAY-nah) A Swahili female name meaning "good."

Male

ZAFI (ZA-fee) A village in Togo.

ZAHUR (ZAH-hoor) Swahili male name meaning "flower."

ZAK (zahk) A river in Cape Province, South Africa that is also known as the River **SAK** (sahk). This 350-mile-long (560 kilometers) river flows through fertile agricultural lands.

ZANAHARY (zah-nah-HAHR-ee)   According to the legends of the Betsileo people of central Madagascar, Zanahary is the creator of the universe and the supreme god.

ZERE (ZUH-ruh)   Amaharic of Ethiopia male name meaning "the seed of, the descendent of." Zere can be used in combination with other names, such as **ZERE YACOB** (ZUH-ruh YAH-kohb) to mean "the descendent of Jacob." Zara Iacob (a variation in spelling) Constantine was emperor of Ethiopia from A.D. 1434–1468 during the Solomonic dynasty.

ZARAMO (zah-RAH-moh)   Zaramo refers to a people of eastern Tanzania, their Bantu language, and their art, which is popular for its Masai statues.

ZEBENJO (zay-BEHN-joh)   Ibo of Nigeria male name meaning "avoid sins."

ZESIRO (zeh-SEE-roh)   A Buganda of Uganda name for the firstborn of twins.

ZIFA (ZEE-fah)   A male name of the Ijaw people of Niger.

ZILI (ZEE-lee)   A Thanga people name for males. Zili is the protagonist of a Thanga folktale called "The Messenger Bird."

ZINDER (ZIN-dur)   An oasis and market town in the Sahel in southern Niger. It was the administrative capital of Niger until 1926 when the capital was moved to Niamey. Zinder is an important staging point for travel across the Sahara Desert. The Cross of Zinder got its name from this town. This cross is a valuable neck pendant worn by Tuareg women and is sometimes traded for cattle. The cross, designed with a circle on top and a phallic protrusion towards the bottom, is a symbol of fertility for both males and females.

ZINGA (ZIN-guh)   A town in the Central African Republic.

ZINJ (zinj)   The ancient Arabic name for East Africa. In July of 1959, when Mary and Louis Leakey discovered a skull more than one-and-one-half million years old in the Olduvai Gorge, Tanzania, they called their find Zinjantropus, meaning "man of Zinj." He was dubbed the "nutcracker man" because of his large teeth.

ZO (zoh)   a) The word used in Liberia for folk or traditional medicine and those who practice it. b) The saying "zo kwe zo" means "all people are created equal" in Sangho, the national language of the Central African Republic.

ZOSER (ZOH-sur)   Zoser I was an Egyptian king of the Third Dynasty, from about 2980–2950 B.C., who made his capital at Memphis. Zoser, described as having African features, is buried at Sakkara in the famous step pyramid. (Pyramids were built by the ancient Egyptians as royal tombs). He was called **TOSORTHROS** (toh-SOR-thras) by the Greeks.

ZUBERI (zoo-BAY-ree)   Swahili male name meaning "strong."

ZULU (zoo-loo) This ethnic group originated in 1807 with Chaka the Zulu. Zulu means "heaven." Over four million Zulu people live in South Africa, mainly in the Natal and Transvaal provinces. Zulu is also the name of their Bantu language, which is a dialect of Nguni and uses some clicking sounds. There is an extensive body of literature in the Zulu language.

ZURI (zoo-ree)   A Kiswahili word for "good" and "beautiful."

APPENDIX A

African Names Used as Surnames

ABBAS — Tanzania
ABELO (ah-BAY-loh) — Zaire
ABIOLO — Nigeria
ACHEBE — (ah-CHAY-bay) — Nigeria
ADENIYI — Nigeria
ADESANYA — Nigeria
ADHOUM (ahd-HOOM) — Tunisia
AFEWORK (AH-fuh-wurk) — Ethiopia
AFRANI — Ghana
AGBEBI —Yoruba of Nigeria
AHANDA (ah-HAHN-dah) — Cameroon
AIDOO (ah-ee-doh) — Ghana
AKII-BUA (ah-kee-BOO-ah) — Kenya
AKINTUNDE — West Africa
AKUFFO — Ghana
ALIER — Dinka of South Sudan
ALUKO — Nigeria
AMADI — Nigeria
ARMAH — Ghana
ATEBA — Cameroon
AWOONOR — Ghana
AZIKIWE — Nigeria
BA (bah) —West Africa
BABANGIDA (bah-bahn-GEE-dah) — Nigeria
BABITO (bah-BEE-toh) — former royal dynasty of the Bunyoro of Uganda
BAHINDA (bah-HEEN-dah) — former royal dynasty of East Africa

150

BAKITA — Sudan
BANKOLE — West Africa
BAREK — Morocco
BARRY — Guinea
BAYESA (bah-EE-sah) — Ethiopia
BAYI — Tanzania
BEAVOGUI — Guinea
BETI — Cameroon
BIKILA (bee-KEE-lah) — Oromo of Ethiopia
BIKO (BEE-koh) — South Africa
BILE (BEE-lay) — Somalia
BIOBAKU — Nigeria
BITOK (BEE-tok) — Kenya
BIWOT (BEE-wot) — Kenya
BIYIDI — Cameroon
BOESAK (BOH-sak) — South Africa
BOL (bohl) — Dinka of South Sudan
BONGO — Gabon
BOSHOSHO (buh-SHOH-shoh) —Tutsi of Rwanda and Burundi
BOULMERKA (bohl-MUR-kuh) — Algeria
BOURGUIBA (bor-GEE-buh) —Tunisia
BUHARI — Nigeria
BUNDU — Sierra Leone
BURJA — Hausa of West Africa
BUSIA (boo-SEE-ah) —West and East Africa
BUTHELEZI (boo-teh-LAY-zee) — South Africa
CABRAL (kuh-BRAHL) — Guinea-Bissau
CAMARA (kah-mah-rah) —West Africa
CHILESHE (chee-LAY-shay) — Zambia
CYILIMA —Tutsi royal family
DADDAH (DAH-dah) — Muslim West Africa
DADIE — Cote D'Ivoire
DAFALLA — Sudan
DALI —Tunisia
DEBY (DEH-bee) — Chad
DEMESSIE (duh-MEE-see) — Ethiopia
DENG (dehng) — Dinka of South Sudan
DIA (DEE-ah) —West Africa
DIAKA (dee-AHK-ah) — Zaire
DIALLO —West Africa

DIBANGO — Cameroon
DIOP (DEE-uhp) — Senegal
DIOR —Wolof of Senegal
DIORI — Niger
DULA (DOO-luh) — Ethiopia
DUNDE — Luo of Kenya
EKWENSI — Nigeria
EMECHETA — Nigeria
EYADEMA —Togo
FUNG (funj) — former Sudanese royal family
GARANE (gahr-AHN-ay) — Somalia
HABE — former royal family of the Hausa of West Africa
HABRE (HAH-bray) — Chad
HAKKI — Egypt
HAMIDOU (hah-MEE-doo) — Ghana
JABAVU — Xhosa of South Africa
JIMOH — Nigeria
KABWE (KAH-bway) — Zaire
KAIGWA (kah-EEG-wuh) — Kenya
KALULE (kah-LOO-lay) — Uganda
KAMWANA — Malawi
KANE — Senegal
KANTE (KAHNT-ay) — Senegal
KARIUKI (kair-ee-OO-kee) — Kikuyu of Kenya
KASAVUBU (kah-sah-VOO-boo) — central Africa
KASHAMURA (kah-shah-MOO-rah) — Zaire
KASSAI — Ethiopia
KAUNDA (kah-OON-dah) — Zambia
KAWAWE (kah-WAH-way) —Tanzania
KAYRA — former royal family of eastern Sudan
KEINO (KAY-noh) — Kenya
KEIRA — royal family of Sudan's Fur people
KEITA (KAY-ee-tah) — Malinke of West Africa dynasty name
KENGA — former royal family of Chad
KENYATTA (kehn-YAH-tuh) — Kikuyu of Kenya
KIBAKI (kee-BAHK-ee) — Kenya
KIBET (ki-BEHT) — Kenya
KILONZO (kee-LOHN-zoh) — Akamba of Kenya
KIMANTHI (ki-MAHN-thee) — Kenya
KIMBANGU (keem-BAHN-goo) — Zaire

KIONGO (kee-OHN-goh) — Kenya
KIPROTICH (KIP-roh-tich) — Kenya
KISIMBA (kee-SEEM-buh) — Zaire
KITUR (ki-TOOR) — Kenya
KOSGEI — Nandi of Kenya
KOUROUMA — Cote D'Ivoire
KUKAH — Nigeria
KULIBALI — Bambara of West Africa
KUNENE — South Africa
KUNTA (KOON-tah) — West African Muslim dynasty
KUTAKE — Namibia
KUTI (KOO-tee) — Nigeria
KWEI (kway) — Ga of Ghana
LALIBELA (lah-lee-BEH-lah) — Ethiopia
LENSHINA (layn-SHEE-nah) — Zambia
LIYONG — Uganda
LONGO-LONGO (LOHN-goh LOHN-goh) — Zaire
LUMUMBA (loo-MOOM-buh) — central Africa
LUSALAH (loo-SAHL-uh) — Kenya
LUSWETI (loo-SWEH-tee) — Kenya
LUTHULI (loo-TOO-lee, loo-THOO-lee) — Zulu of South Africa
MAATHAI (mah-THIGH) — Kikuyu of Kenya
MAINA (MIGH-nuh) — Kikuyu of Kenya
MAKANDA (mah-KAHN-dah) — Zaire
MAKEBA (may-KAY-bah) — South Africa
MAKIADI (mah-kee-AH-dee) — Zaire
MAKONI (mah-KOHN-ee) — Zaire
MANDELA (mahn-DEHL-ah) — South Africa
MARENGO — Namibia
MARGAI — West Africa
MASEKELA (mah-seh-KAY-lah) — South Africa
MATETE (mah-TAY-tay) — Zambia
MATIBA (mah-TEE-buh) — Kenya
MATIKU (mah-TEE-koo) — Kenya
MATLAPIN — Botswana
MAZRUI (mah-zuh-ROO-ee) — royal family from the east coast of Kenya
MBARGA — West Africa
MBOYA (m-BOY-uh) — Kenya
MIKA (MEE-kuh) — Kikuyu of Kenya

MILONGO (mee-LOHN-goh) — Congo
MINAH — Sierra Leone
MOFOLO — Lesotho
MONENGA (moh-NAYN-gah) — central Africa
MORCELI (mor-seh-LEE) — Morocco
MOUTAWAKEL — Morocco
MUBARAK (moo-BAHR-ahk) — Egypt
MUHAVI (moo-HAHV-ee) — Kenya
MUTARA — Tutsi royal family
MUKABI (moo-KAH-bee) — Luya of Kenya
MUTOLO (moo-TOH-loh) — Mozambique
MWACHOFI (mwah-CHOH-fee) — Kenya
MWALE (MWAH-lay) — Kenya
MWANGI (MWAHN-gee) — Kikuyu of Kenya
MWINSHESHE (mwin-SHAY-shay) — Tanzania
MWINYI (MWIN-yee) — Tanzania
MZALI — Tunisia
NGALA (n-GAH-lah) — Kenya
NHONGO (n-HOHN-goh) — Zimbabwe
NKOMO (n-KOH-moh) — Matebele of Zimbabwe
NKOSI — South Africa
NKRUMAH (n-KROO-mah) — Akan of Ghana
NYERERE (nyair-AIR-ay) — Tanzania
NYIRENDA — Malawi
NYONI — Zimbabwe
NZIBO (n-ZEE-boh) — Kenya
OBASANJO — Nigeria
ODINGA (oh-DING-uh) — Luo of Kenya
OFFEI (oh-FAY) — Ghana
OFFRATA (oh-FRAH-tah) — Ghana
OKARA — Nigeria
OKINO (oh-KEEN-oh) — Uganda
OKOTH (oh-KOHTH) — Uganda
OMOLO (oh-MOH-loh) — Kenya
OSEWE (oh-SAY-way) — Kenya
OUSMANE — West Africa
OWITI (oh-WEE-tee) — Kenya
OYONO — Cameroon
RAMAPHOSA — South Africa
RONO (ROH-noh) — Kenya

RUMFA — Hausa of West Africa
RUSERE (roo-SAY-ray) — Mozambique
SAITOTI (sigh-TOH-tee) — Masai of Kenya
SARUCHERA — (sah-roo-CHAY-rah) Zimbabwe
SASSI — Tunisia
SEBANGENI (say-bahn-GEHN-ee) — Tutsi of Rwanda and Burundi
SEMBENE (saym-BAY-nay) — Ghana
SENGHOR (sehn-GAWR) — Senegal
SHIKUKU (shee-KOO-koo) — Kenya
SIBANDA (see-BAHN-dah) — Zimbabwe
SIYON — Ethiopia
SOLAJA — Nigeria
SOYINKA — Nigeria
SSEMWANGA (say-MWAHN-guh) — Uganda
SUHUL — Ethiopia
TAMBO (TAM-boh) — South Africa
TANUI (tah-NOO-ee) Kenya
THUKU (THOO-koo) — Kenya
TOURE (too-RAY) — Guinea
TRUDO — Benin
TULU (TOO-loo) — Ethiopia
TUTU (TOO-too) — South Africa and West Africa
WANDABWA (wahn-DAHB-wah) — Kenya
WANYIKA (wahn-YEE-kuh) — Tanzania
WOLDE — Ethiopia
WORKU (WUR-koo) — Ethiopia
YUHI (YOO-hee) — former Tutsi royal family
ZAGWE (ZAHG-way) — former royal dynasty of Ethiopia

APPENDIX B

Leaders of Modern Africa

Algeria

Ahmed Ben Bella	1963–1965
Houari Boumedienne	1965–1978
Chadli Bendjedid	1979–1992
Mohamed Boudiaf	1992–present

Angola

Agostinho Neto	1975–1979
José Eduardo dos Santos	1979–present

Benin

Hubert Maga	1960–1963/1970–1972
Sourou-Migan Apithy	1964–1965
Christophe Soglo	1965–1967
Emile-Derlin Zinsou	1968–1969
Justin Ahomadegbe; Apithy; Maga	1970–1972
Mathieu Kerekou	1972–1991
Nicéphore Soglo	1991–present

Botswana

Seretse M. Khama	1966–1980
Quett K. J. Masire	1980–present

Burkino Faso

Maurice Yaméogo	1960–1966
Sangoulé Lamizana	1966–1980
Sayé Zerbo	1980–1982
Jean-Baptiste Ouedraogo	1982–1983
Thomas Sankara	1983–1987
Blaise Compaore	1987–present

Burundi

Mwami (King) Mwambutsa IV	1962–1966
Mwami (King) Natare V	1966
Michel Micombero	1966–1976
Jean-Baptiste Bagaza	1976–1987
Pierre Buyoya	1987–present

Cameroon

Ahmadou Babatoura Ahidjo	1960–1982
Paul Biya	1982–present

Cape Verde

Aristides María Pereira	1975–1991
António Mascarenhas Monteiro	1991–present

Central African Republic

David Dacko	1960–1966/1979–1981
Jean-Bedel Bokassa	1966–1979
André-Dieudonné Kolingba	1981–present

Chad

Francois (Ngarta) Tombalbaye	1959–1975
Félix Malloum	1975–1979
Goukhouni Oueddei	1979–1982
Hissein Habre	1982–1990
Idriss Deby	1990–present

Comoros

Prince Jaffar	1975
Ahmed Abdallah Abderemane	1975/1978–1989
Ali Soilih	1976–1978
Said Mohamed Djohar	1989–present

Congo

Fulbert Youlou	1960–1963
Alphonse Massamba-Debat	1963–1968
Marien Ngouabi	1969–1977
Joachim Yhombi-Opango	1977–1979
Denis Sassou-Nguesso	1979–1991
Andre Milongo	1991–present

Cote D'Ivoire

Félix Houphouet-Boigny	1960–present

Djibouti

Hassan Gouled Aptidon	1977–present

Egypt

Muhammad Nagib	1953–1955
Gamal Abdel Nasser	1956–1970
Muhammad Ahmad Anwar al-Sadat	1970–1981
Muhammad Hosni Mubarak	1981–present

Equatorial Guinea

Macie Nguema Biyogo Ñegue Ndong	1968–1979
Teodoro Obiang Nguema Mbasogo	1979–present

Ethiopia

Haile Mariam Selassie I	1930–1974
(Ras Tafari Makonnen)	
Mengistu Haile-Mariam	1974–1991
Meles Zenawi	1991–present

Gabon

Léon M'Ba	1960–1967
El Hadj Omar Bongo	1967–present

Gambia

Alhaji Dawda Kairaba Jawara	1970–present

Ghana

Kwame N. Nkrumah	1957–1966
Joseph A. Ankrah	1966–1969
Kofi A. Busia	1969–1972
Ignatius Kutu Acheampong	1972–1978
Frederick W. F. Akuffo	1978–1979
Hilla Limann	1979–1981
Jerry John Rawlings	1982–present

Guinea

Ahmed Sékou Toure	1958–1984
Lansana Beavogui	1984
Lansana Conte	1984–present

Guinea-Bissau

Luis de Almeida Cabral	1974–1980
João Bernardo Vieira	1980–present

Kenya

Jomo Kenyatta	1963–1978
Daniel Teroitich arap Moi	1978–present

Lesotho

King Moshoeshoe II	1966–1990
King Letsie III	1990–present

Liberia

Garrett W. Gibson	1900–1904
Arthur Barclay	1904–1912
Daniel E. Howard	1912–1920
Charles D. B. King	1920–1930
Edwin Barclay	1930–1944
William V. S. Tubman	1944–1971
William Richard Tolbert, Jr.	1971–1980
Samuel Kanyon Doe	1980–1990
Amos Sawyer	1990–present

Libya

Emir Muhammad Idris al-Sanussi (King Idris I)	1951–1969
Mu'ammar Abu Minyar al-Qadhafi	1969–present

Madagascar

Philibert Tsiranana	1960–1972
Richard Ratsimandrava	1972
Gabriel Ramanantsoa	1972–1975
Didier Ratsiraka	1975–present

Malawi

Ngwazi Hastings Kamuzu Banda   1964–present

Mali

Modibo Keita   1960–1968
Moussa Traore   1968–1991
Amadou Toumani Toure   1991–1992
Alpha Oumar Konare   1992–present

Mauritania

Moktar Ould Daddah   1960–1978
Mustapha Ould Salek   1978–1979
Mohamed Mahmoud Ould Ahmed Louly 1979–1980
Mohamed Khouana Ould Haidalla   1980–1984
Maaouya Ould Sid Ahmed Taya   1984–present

Mauritius

Seewoosagur Ramgoolam   1968–1982
Aneerood Jugnauth   1982–present

Morocco

King Mohamed V   1956–1961
King Hassan II   1961–present

Mozambique

Samora Machel   1975–1986
Joaquim Alberto Chissano   1986–present

Namibia

Sam Shafilshuna Nujoma   1990–present

Niger

Hamani Diori	1959–1974
Seyni Kountché	1974–1987
Ali Saibou	1987–present

Nigeria

Nnamdi Azikiwe	1963–1966
Johnson T.U. Aguiyi-Ironsi	1966
Yakubu Gowon	1966–1975
Murtala Ramat Muhammad	1975–1976
Olusegun Obasanjo	1976–1979
Alhaji Shehu Shagari	1979–1983
Muhammadu Buhari	1984–1985
Ibrahim Babangida	1985–present

Rwanda

Grégoire Kayibanda	1961–1973
Juvénal Habyarimana	1973–present

Sao Tome E Principe

Manuel Pinto de Costa	1975–1991
Miguel Anjos da Cunha Lisboa Travoada	1991–present

Senegal

Léopold Sédar Senghor	1960–1980
Abdou Diouf	1981–present

Seychelles

James Richard Mancham	1976–1977
France Albert Rene	1977–present

Sierra Leone

Milton Margai	1961–1964
Albert M. Margai	1964–1967
Andrew Juxon-Smith	1967–1968
Siaka Probyn Stevens	1969–1985
Joseph Saidu Momoh	1985–present

Somalia

Abdirashid Ali Shermarke	1967–1969
Mohamed Siad Barre	1969–1991
Ali Mahdi Mohamed	1991–present

South Africa

Hendrik F. Verwoerd	1958–1966
Balthazar J. Vorster	1966–1978
Pieter Willem Botha	1978–1989
Frederik Willem DeKlerk	1989–present

Sudan

Ibrahim Abbud	1958–1964
Muhammad Ahmad Mahgub	1964–1969
Ja'far Muhammad Numayri	1969–1985
Abdel Rahman Siwar al-Dahab	1985–1986
Sadiq al-Mahdi	1986–1989
Umar Hassan Ahmad al-Bashir	1989–present

Swaziland

King Sobhuza II	1966–1982
Queen Ntombi Thwala	1982–1986
King Mswati III	1986–present

Tanzania

Julius Kambarage Nyerere	1962–1985
Ali Hassan Mwinyi	1985–present

Togo

Sylvanus Olympio	1961–1963
Nicolas Grunitzky	1963–1967
Gnassingbé Eyadema	1967–present

Tunisia

Habib Bourguiba	1957–1987
Zine El-Abidine Ben Ali	1987–present

Uganda

Kabbaka Yekka (King Edward Mutesa)	1962–1966
Milton Obote	1966–1971/1980–1985
Idi Amin Dada	1971–1979
Usefu Lule	1979
Godfrey Binaisa	1979
Tito Okello Lutwa	1985–1986
Yoweri Kaguta Musevini	1986–present

Zaire

Patrice Lumumba	1960–1961
Moise Tshombe	1964–1965
Mobutu Sese Seko Kuku Ngbendu Wa Za Banga	1965–present

Zambia

Kenneth David Kaunda	1964–1992

Zimbabwe

Canaan Sodindo Banana	1980
Robert Gabriel Mugabe	1980–present

APPENDIX C

Suggested Reading

AFRICAN WRITERS

Achebe, Chinua. *A Man of the People*. New York: Anchor Books, 1966.

———. *Girls at War and Other Stories*. New York: Doubleday, 1973.

———. *Christmas in Biafra and Other Poems*. New York: Doubleday, 1973.

———. *Anthills of the Savannah*. New York: Anchor Press, 1987.

Beti, Mongo. *Mission to Kala*. London: Heinemann, 1958.

———. *King Lazarus*. London: Heinemann, 1960.

Diop, Cheikh Anta. *The African Origin of Civilization: Myth or Reality*. Chicago: Lawrence Hill Books, 1974.

Ekwensi, Cyprian. *Jagua Nana*. London: Heinemann, 1961.

———. *Lokotown and Other Stories*. London: Heinemann, 1966.

———. *Survive the Peace*. London: Heinemann, 1976.

Emecheta, Buchi. *The Rape of Shavi*. New York: G. Braziller, 1976.

———. *The Bride Price*. New York: G. Braziller, 1976.

———. *Second-Class Citizen*. New York: G. Braziller, 1982.

Fannon, Frantz. *The Wretched of the Earth*. New York: Grove Press, 1963.

———. *Black Skin, White Masks*. New York: Grove Press, 1967.

Farah, Nuruddin. *Sweet and Sour Milk*. London: Allison & Busby, 1979.

———. *Maps*. New York: Pantheon Books, 1986.

Gordimer, Nadine. *A Sport of Nature*. New York: Knopf, 1987.

———. *The Conservationist*. New York: Viking Press, 1974.

———. *July's People*. New York: Viking Press, 1981.

———. *Jump and Other Stories*. New York: Farrar, Straus, Giroux, 1991.

Head, Bessie. *Maru*. New York: McCall Publishing Co., 1971.

———. *A Question of Power*. London: Heinemann, 1974.

———. *When Rain Clouds Gather*. New York: McCall Publishing Co., 1968.

Kane, Cheikh Hamidou. *Ambiguous Adventure*. London: Heinemann, 1972.

Karodia, Farida. *Coming Home and Other Stories*. London: Heinemann, 1988.

Kenyatta, Jomo. *Facing Mount Kenya*. New York: Vintage Books, 1965.

La Guma, Alex. *In the Fog of the Season's End*. New York: Third Press, 1972.

_____.*A Walk in the Night*. London: Heinemann, 1967.

Laye, Camara. *Dark Child*. New York: Hill and Wang, 1954.

_____. *The Radiance of the King*. New York: Vintage, 1989.

_____. *Guardian of the Word*. New York: Aventura, 1980.

Materra, Don. *Sophia Town: Coming of Age in South Africa*. Boston: Beacon Press, 1987.

Mphahlele, Ezekiel. *Voices in the Whirlwind*. New York: Hill and Wang, 1972.

_____.*Renewal Time*. Louisiana: Reader's International, 1988.

Wicomb, Zoe. *You Can't Get Lost in Cape Town*. New York: Pantheon Books, 1987.

ADVENTURE/JOURNEY/FICTION

Boyles, Denis. *African Lives*. New York: Weidenfeld & Nicolson, 1988.

Drew, Eileen. *Blue Taxis*. Minnesota: Milkweed Editions, 1989.

Durrell, Lawrence. *Clea*. London: Faber and Faber, 1960.

Hallet, Jean-Pierre. *Congo Kitabu*. Connecticut: Fawcett Crest Book, 1964.

Harris, Eddy L. *Native Stranger*. New York: Simon & Schuster, 1992.

Hillaby, John. *Journey to the Jade Sea*. London: Paladin Graftin Books, 1964.

Lovell, Mary S., compiled. *The Splendid Outcast: The African Stories of Beryl Markham*. London: Arrow Books, 1987.

Markham, Beryl. *West With the Night*. London: Penguin Books, 1942.

Moorehead, Alan. *The Blue Nile*. New York: Harper & Row Publishers, 1962.

Naipaul, Shiva. *North of South*. New York: Penguin Books, 1978.

Naipaul, V. S. *A Bend in the River*. New York: Vintage Books, 1979.

Pye-Smith, Charlie. *The Other Nile*. New York: Penguin Books, 1987.

Thesinger, Wilfred. *The Life of My Choice*. Glasglow: William Collins, 1987.

Thomas, Maria. *Come to Africa and Save Your Marriage*. New York: Soho Press, 1987.

ACADEMIC/OTHER

Abrahams, Roger D. *African Folktales*. New York: Pantheon Books, 1983.

Anderson, Jon Lee and Scott. *War Zones*. New York: Dodd, Mead & Company, 1988.

Courtney-Clarke, Margaret. *African Canvas; The Art of West African Women*. New York: Rizzoli, 1990.

Davidson, Basil. *African Civilization Revisited*. Trenton, New Jersey: Africa World Press, 1991.

Deng, Francis Mading. *The Dinka of Sudan*. Illinois: Waveland Press, Inc., 1972.

Graham, Ronnie. *The Da Capo Guide to Contemporary African Music*. New York: Da Capo Press, 1988.

Gruber, Ruth. *Rescue: The Exodus of the Ethiopian Jews*. New York: Atheneum, 1987.

Hamm, Charles. *Afro-American Music, South Africa, and Apartheid*. City University of New York: Institute for Studies in American Music, 1988.

Harris, Joseph E. *Africans and Their History*. Mentor Books, New York: Penguin Group, 1987.

Hooper, Ed. *Slim*. London: The Bodley Head, 1990.

Jablow, Alta. *Yes & No: The Intimate Folklore of Africa*. New York: Horizon Press, 1961.

Klein, Leonard S., editor. *African Literature in the 20th Century*. New York: The Ungar Publishing Company, 1986.

Lamb, David. *The Africans*. New York: Vintage Books, 1983.

Martin, Phyllis and Patrick O'Meara. *Africa*. Bloomington: Indiana University Press, 1986.

Sertima, Ivan Van, editor. *Black Women in Antiquity*. London: Transaction Books, 1988.

Stapelton, Chris and May Chris. *African Rock: The Pop Music of a Continent*. New York: Obelisk/Dutton, 1990.

167

Vansina, Jan. *Art History in Africa.* Madison: University of Wisconsin Press, 1984.

CHILDREN'S BOOKS

Borden, Beatrice. *Wild Animals of Africa.* New York: Random House, 1982.

Caldwell, John C. *Let's Visit Middle Africa: East Africa, Central Africa, Zaire.* New York: John Day, 1970.

Haskins, Jim. *Count Your Way Through Africa.* Minneapolis: Carolrhoda Books, Inc.

Kallen, Stuart A. *The Lost Kingdoms of Africa: Black Africa Before 1600.* Minnesota: Abdo and Daughters, 1990.

Lewin, Hugh. *Jafta-The Journey.* Minneapolis: Carolrhoda Books, Inc., 1984.

_____.*Jafta-The Town.* Minneapolis: Carolrhoda Books, Inc., 1984.

Margolies, Barbara A. *Rehema's Journey: A Visit in Tanzania.* New York: Scholastic Inc., 1990.

Ward, Leila. *I Am Eyes: Ni Macho.* New York: Scholastic Inc.,1987.

Bibliography

Ashley, Leonard R. N. *What's In a Name?*. Maryland: Genealogical Publishing Co., Inc., 1989.

Banks, Arthur S., editor. *Political Handbook of the World 1991*. New York: CSA Publications, 1991.

Bergman, Billy. *Goodtime: Emerging African Pop*. New York: Quill, 1985.

Boyle, Bernadette and Ellen Knutson, editors. *Hildebrand's Travel Guide to Kenya*. K&G Karto & Grafik, West Germany: Verlagsgesellschaft, 1987.

Browder, Sue. *The New Age Baby Name Book*. New York: Workman Publishing, 1987.

Canby, Courtland. *A Guide to the Archeological Sites of Israel, Egypt and North Africa*. New York: Facts on File Publications, 1990.

Chilcote, Ronald H. *Portuguese Africa*. New Jersey: Prentice-Hall, Inc., 1967.

Chuks-Orji, Ogonna. *Names From Africa*. Chicago: Johnson Publishing, 1972.

Cotterell, Arthur. *A Dictionary of World Mythology*. New York: G. P. Putnam and Sons, 1980.

Crewe, Quentin. *In Search of the Sahara*. New York: MacMillan Publishing Co., 1983.

Crowther, Geoff. *Africa on a Shoestring*. Australia: Lonely Planet Publications, 1986.

Davidson, Basil. *African Kingdoms*. New York: Time-Life Books, 1966.

Delaney, John J. *Dictionary of Saints*. New York: Doubleday and Company, 1980.

Douglas, J. D., editor. *New 20th-Century Encyclopedia of Religious Knowledge*. Grand Rapids, Michigan: Baker Book House, 1991.

Ellefson, Connie Lockhart. *The Melting Pot Book of Baby Names*. Virginia: Betterway Publications, Inc., 1990.

Encyclopedia of Art. vol. 1, New York: McGraw-Hill Book Company, Inc., 1968.

Ferguson, Everett, editor. *Encyclopedia of Early Christianity*. New York: Garland Publishing, Inc., 1990.

Fields, Maxine. *Baby Names From Around the World.* New York: Pocket Books, 1985.

Fisher, Angela. *Africa Adorned.* London: Collins Harvill, 1987.

Freeman-Grenville, G.S.P. *The New Atlas of African History.* New York: Simon & Schuster, 1991.

Fuglestad, Finn. *A History of Niger 1850–1960.* Cambridge University Press, 1983.

Gallman, Kuki. *I Dreamed of Africa.* New York: Viking, 1991.

Hakim, Dawud. *Arabic Names and Other African Names With Their Meanings.* Philadelphia: Hakim's Publications, 1970.

Jablow, Alta. *Yes & No: The Intimate Folklore of Africa.* New York: Horizon Press, 1961.

Julyan, Robert Hixson. *Mountain Names.* Seattle: The Mountaineers, 1984.

Kane, Robert S. *Africa A to Z.* New York: Doubleday and Company Inc., 1972.

Katzner, Kenneth. *The Languages of the World.* New York: Funk & Wagnalls, 1975.

King, Anita. *Quotations in Black.* Westport, Connecticut: Greenwood Press, 1981.

Kolatch, Alfred J. *The Name Dictionary.* New York: Jonathan David, 1967.

Lansky, Bruce and Vicky. *The Best Baby Name Book in the Whole Wide World.* Deephaven, Minnesota: Meadow Book Press, 1979.

Lanting, Frans. *A World Out of Time: Madagascar.* New York: Aperture Foundation, Inc., 1990.

Madubuike, Ihechekwu. *A Handbook of African Names.* Washington, D.C.: Three Continents Press, 1976.

Mathews, C. M. *Place Names in the English-Speaking World.* New York: Charles Scribner's Sons, 1972.

Mazrui, Ali A. *The Africans: A Triple Heritage.* Boston: Little, Brown and Company, 1986.

Menke, Frank G. *The Encyclopedia of Sports.* New York: A. S. Barnes and Company, 1977.

Moorehead, Alan. *The Blue Nile.* New York: Harper and Row Publishers, 1962.

Moss, Joyce and George Wilson. *Africans South of the Sahara.* Detroit: Gale Research Inc., 1991.

Moss, Joyce and George Wilson. *The Middle East and North Africa.* Detroit: Gale Research Inc., 1991.

Naylor, Kim. *Discovery Guide to West Africa*. London: Michael Haag, 1989.

Reed, W. L. and M. J. Bristow, editors. *National Anthems of the World*. London: Blanford Press, 1987.

Robinson, H. S. and K. Wilson. *The Encyclopedia of Myths and Legends of All Nations*. London: Kaye & Ward Ltd., 1950.

Room, Adrian. *Place-Names of the World*. Australia: Angus & Robertson Publishers, 1987.

Shoumatoff, Alex. *African Madness*. New York: Alfred A. Knopf, 1988.

Snowden, Frank M. *Blacks in Antiquity*. Massachusetts: Harvard University Press, 1970.

Suttles, Sherry A. and Billye Suttles-Graham. *Fielding's Africa South of the Sahara*. New York: William Morrow and Co., 1986.

Taylor, Isaac. *Names and Their Histories*. London: Rivingtons, 1988.

The Encyclopedia of Africa. New York/London: Franklin Watts, Inc., 1976.

Thompson, Lloyd A. *Romans and Blacks*. Norman, Oklahoma: University of Oklahoma Press, 1989.

Vitaliano, Dorothy B. *Legends of the Earth: Their Geological Origin*. Bloomington: Indiana University Press, 1973.

Wilson, Charles Morrow. *Liberia: Black Africa in Microcosm*. New York: Harper and Row, 1971.

More Books of African-American Interest
From Carol Publishing Group

Carol Publishing Group proudly publishes dozens of books of African-American interest. From history to contemporary issues facing Black Americans and popular culture, these books take a compelling look at the African-American experience.

<u>Selected titles include:</u> • **The African-American Health Book** • **The African-American Books of Days** • **The African Cookbook: Menus and Recipes From 11 African Countries and the Island of Zanzibar** • **African Names: Names From the African Continent for Children and Adults** • **Afro-American History: The Modern Era** • **The Autobiography of Jack Johnson: In the Ring, and Out** • **Black Hollywood: The Black Performer in Motion Pictures, Volume 1 & 2** • **Black Is the Color of My TV Tube** • **The Black 100: A Ranking of the Most Influential African-Americans, Past and Present** • **Black Robes, White Justice: Why Our Legal System Doesn't Work for Blacks** • **Caroling Dusk: An Anthology of Verse by Black Poets** • **Classic African Children's Stories** • **Clotel: Or, the President's Daughter** • **A Complete History of the Negro Leagues, 1884 - 1955** • **The Ditchdigger's Daughters: A Black Family's Astonishing Success Story** • **A Documentary History of the Negro People in the United States, Volumes 1 through 7** • **First Lady of Song: Ella Fitzgerald For the Record** • **Good Morning Revolution: Selected Poetry and Prose of Langston Hughes** • **Harriet Tubman: The Moses of Her People** • **A History of the Negro Leagues, 1884 to 1955** • **Introduction to African Civilizations** • **Langston Hughes: Before and Beyond Harlem** • **Life & Times of Frederick Douglass** • **Lyrics of Lowly Life: The Poetry of Paul Laurence Dunbar** • **Man, God and Civilization** • **Negro in the South** • **The Negro Novelist: 1940-1950** • **Negrophobia: An Urban Parable** • **Negro Slave Songs in the United States** • **The New Soul-Food Cookbook** • **1,001 African Names** • **Paul Robeson Speaks: Writings, Speeches and Interviews 1918-1974** • **Prisoners of Our Past: A Critical Look at Self-Defeating Attitudes Within the Black Community** • **Racism and Psychiatry** • **Repeal of the Blues: How Black Entertainers Influenced Civil Rights** • **Revelations: The Autobiography of Alvin Ailey** • **Soul in Management: How African-American Managers Can Thrive in the Competitive Corporate Enviornment** • **Thurgood Marshall: Warrior at the Bar, Rebel on the Bench** • **To Be Free: A Volume of Studies in Afro-American History** • **Up From Slavery** • **The Way It Was in the South: The Black Experience in Georgia** • **What Color Is Your God?: Black Consciousness and the Christian Faith** • **The Whole World in His Hands: A Pictorial Biography of Paul Robeson** • **Why Black People Tend to Shout: Cold Facts and Wry Views from a Black Man's World** • **Work, Sister, Work: How Black Women Can Get Ahead in the Workplace**

Ask for these African-American Interest books at your bookstore. To place an order, or for more information, or a free descriptive brochure, call 1-800-447-BOOK or send your name and address to Carol Publishing Group, 120 Enterprise Ave., Dept. 1737, Secaucus, NJ 07094. Books subject to availability